Fostering Teachers' Mental Health

Valeria Cavioni

Fostering Teachers' Mental Health

Evidence from Theory, Research, and Practice

palgrave
macmillan

Valeria Cavioni
Department of Humanities and Social Sciences
Universitas Mercatorum
Rome, Italy

ISBN 978-3-031-92570-2 ISBN 978-3-031-92571-9 (eBook)
https://doi.org/10.1007/978-3-031-92571-9

This Palgrave Macmillan imprint is published by the registered company Springer Nature Switzerland AG.
The registered company address is: Gewerbestrasse 11, 6330 Cham, Switzerland

To those who have stood by my side, who have cared for me with kindness and love, who have encouraged me to keep going despite the challenges. To those who have given me their trust, their warmth, and their unwavering support, expecting nothing in return. This book is for you.

Foreword

Teaching is a profession deeply embedded in human relationships and continuously influenced by the social, economic, cultural, and technological changes taking place in society, making it a demanding and challenging profession, even if a rewarding one as well. It is thus not surprising that the current focus on the promotion of well-being and mental health in schools in Europe, North America, Australia, and other parts of the globe has been addressing not only the well-being of students but that of the educators themselves as well. Any school initiative in the promotion of mental health and well-being needs to start with that of the adults. It is difficult for struggling, tired, stressed, and burnt-out teachers to provide adequate care and support to students. On the other hand, adequately supported teachers who are managing well the challenges and demands of their profession are in a unique position to support the education and development of their students. They serve as a source of inspiration to their students through their caring relationships, mentoring, and role modelling of positive academic and social attitudes and behaviours.

Fostering Teachers' Mental Health: Evidence from Theory, Research, and Practice thus comes at a very opportune time as schools across the globe are increasing their efforts to promote and protect the mental health and well-being of their community. In this well-researched book, drawing on extensive literature as well as practice, Valeria Cavioni provides a solid foundation of the theory, research and practice in teacher well-being and mental health. The book uniquely integrates theory and practice, balancing various theories and frameworks from mental health, social and emotional learning and resilience, amongst others, with practical implications for the promotion and protection of mental health, including examples from the author's own work. The book provides a comprehensive theoretical background to unravel the complexities of teachers' mental health, followed by an in-depth discussion of classroom relationships and teachers' mental health, with a particular focus on the dynamics of the teacher-student relationship. It concludes with a discussion of evidence-based programmes and interventions in teacher mental health, including two programmes the author herself was involved in.

In this highly engaging and informative book, Valeria Cavioni invites us to take an in-depth look at teacher mental health within the current social, economic, cultural, and technological changes, and explore how it may be actively promoted and protected. Amongst the various strengths and innovations of the book is the presentation of various theoretical frameworks of teacher mental health, including the author's own; a review of the research on teachers' mental health and respective interventions; findings from the author's own research capturing the voices of the teachers themselves on classroom relationships; and the presentation of two European programmes on teacher mental health in which the author was involved. This book is highly relevant to the current realities in the teaching profession and should serve as an invaluable resource not only to academia and initial teacher education programmes, but especially for schools and teacher communities in their efforts to promote and protect the mental health of their staff.

University of Malta
Msida, Malta

Carmel Cefai

Acknowledgements

This book is born from the encounters, dialogues, and experiences I have had with countless teachers over the years. From my own education to my work as a researcher and trainer, I have been fortunate to meet extraordinary educators in diverse educational settings, each of them leaving a profound impact on my understanding of teaching and learning.

To all the teachers who have generously shared their stories, challenges, and insights with me: thank you. Our relationship has never been one-directional. If, in my role, I have had the opportunity to guide and support you, I have equally learned from your dedication, resilience, and passion. Every conversation, every reflection, and every challenge we have faced together has enriched me just as much as I hope it has supported you.

It is with deep gratitude that I dedicate these words to you, teachers who inspire, shape, and transform not only the lives of students but also those who, like me, have had the privilege of walking alongside you on this journey.

Competing Interests The author has no competing interests to declare that are relevant to the content of this manuscript.

Contents

Abbreviations

CASEL	Collaborative for Academic, Social, and Emotional Learning
CD-RISC	Connor-Davidson Resilience Scale
CLASS	Classroom Assessment Scoring System
COVID	Coronavirus Disease
DSM-5-TR	Diagnostic and Statistical Manual of Mental Disorders, Fifth Edition Text Revision
ICD-11	International Classification of Diseases, 11th Revision
OSTES	Ohio State Teacher Efficacy Scale
OWC	Online Wellbeing Course
PROMEHS	Promoting Mental Health at Schools
PTSD	Post-Traumatic Stress Disorder
SECTRS	Social and Emotional Competence of Teachers
SEL	Social and Emotional Learning
T2Be	Teaching to Be
TTB	Teacher-Targeted Bullying
WHO	World Health Organization

List of Figures

List of Tables

List of Boxes

1

Introduction

Abstract This chapter explores teacher mental health as a fundamental yet often overlooked dimension of educational quality and sustainability. Grounded in the relational and emotional nature of teaching, it emphasizes that the heart of schooling lies not only in knowledge transmission but also in the meaningful human connections forged in classrooms. The chapter highlights the dual impact of teacher-student relationships, showing their potential to promote or hinder student development and teacher well-being. It advocates for educational policies that centre on the mental health of teachers, recognizing that ensuring their psychological support is essential to creating equitable, effective, and nurturing learning environments.

Keywords Teacher mental health • Teacher-student relationships • Teaching • Work-related stress • Educational policy

> The true heart of the school is made up of lesson time that can be adventures, meetings, deep intellectual and emotional experiences.
>
> Because what remains of school [...] is the beauty of the lesson hour.
>
> Can a lesson hour open a world? It can always be the time for a real encounter.

V. Cavioni, *Fostering Teachers' Mental Health*,
https://doi.org/10.1007/978-3-031-92571-9_1

> A good teacher. Isn't it someone who knows how to create new worlds, isn't someone who still believes that a lesson hour can change a life? (Recalcati, 2014, p. 8)

These words by Recalcati, a globally recognized psychoanalyst and author, capture the profound essence of teaching, emphasizing the belief that a single lesson, conversation, or moment of connection can open new worlds and shape a student's life. Beyond the rigour of curricula and the pressures of standardized assessments, the true legacy of education lies in the relationships that develop between teachers and students. These connections extend beyond the classroom, leaving a lasting impact on both learners and educators. If we pause and reflect, many of us can recall a teacher who changed the way we saw ourselves, who recognized potential we had yet to acknowledge, who offered encouragement in moments of doubt, and who, through their presence, taught us not just about a subject, but about resilience, curiosity, and the courage to aspire.

Years later, when we unexpectedly encounter these teachers, perhaps on the street, at a chance event, or even through a message sent long after graduation, an overwhelming mix of nostalgia, gratitude, and emotion resurfaces. We find ourselves eager to share who we have become, our paths, our successes, and our challenges, as if seeking their silent confirmation that their lessons mattered. Their words, their gestures, and the way they guided us through our formative years remain woven into our identities. And these encounters are just as profoundly moving for teachers. The joy of seeing former students grow into confident adults, forging their own paths in life, is one of the most rewarding aspects of the profession. A simple *thank you*, a glimpse of the person a student has become, is often more validating than any external recognition. At that moment, the exhaustion, the emotional toll, and the daily struggles fade away, leaving behind the quiet certainty that their work held meaning.

Yet, this deeply human dimension of teaching, the power of relationships, the weight of responsibility, and the emotional investment, often goes unspoken in conversations about education. Teaching is not merely the transmission of knowledge; it is an act of presence, of connection, of shaping lives. However, while much attention has been devoted to the role of teachers in fostering student well-being, there has been far less recognition of what sustains the well-being of teachers themselves. Educators are expected to be resilient, empathetic, and engaged, yet the very nature of their work exposes them to chronic stress, emotional exhaustion, and psychological strain. The mental health of teachers is often overlooked in discussions about school well-being, despite the growing body of research indicating that their emotional state profoundly impacts not only their personal and professional lives but also the quality of the educational environment they create.

Building on this foundation, the first chapter of this book explores teacher mental health as a complex, multidimensional construct, examining risk factors such as work-related stress, burnout, post-traumatic stress disorder, bullying, and emotional abuse from school leadership, while also considering protective factors like resilience and social and emotional competencies.

The second chapter examines the crucial role of teacher-student relationships in shaping students' cognitive, social, emotional, and academic development. It explores how emotionally supportive interactions contribute to self-regulation, a sense of community, and academic achievement, while also influencing classroom dynamics and peer relationships. Additionally, the chapter presents a qualitative study analysing teachers' recollections of their own school experiences, offering insights into how these formative interactions impact their educational paths and professional identity.

Finally, the third chapter examines intervention programmes, highlighting how structured initiatives can equip teachers with the necessary skills and support to safeguard their psychological well-being. It presents two successful European Commission co-funded programmes, Promoting Mental Health at Schools (PROMEHS) and Teaching to Be (T2Be). The chapter emphasizes the importance of integrating teacher mental health initiatives into broader educational policies, ensuring their long-term sustainability and systemic impact.

This book seeks to bridge a critical gap by offering a comprehensive, research-informed exploration of teachers' mental health, highlighting the crucial role of school-based interventions that prioritize teacher well-being. It challenges the traditional perception of education as solely academic, instead emphasizing its nature as a relational and emotional ecosystem where teacher well-being is as fundamental as student success. By refocusing attention on teacher-centred interventions, this book acknowledges that teaching carries both protective factors and enriching experiences, such as the meaningful relationships educators build with their students, which can enhance their psychological health. However, it also aims to shed light on less explored and often stigmatized issues related to teacher mental health. Despite its profound impact, the well-being of educators is frequently overlooked, leaving its darker aspects unaddressed.

Among these, the book investigates work-related stress and burnout, which can erode motivation, resilience, and engagement. It also examines bullying experienced by teachers at the hands of students and emotional abuse inflicted by school leadership, two phenomena that remain under-reported and inadequately addressed. These issues are often dismissed or minimized due to deep-rooted stigma—the belief that teachers, as authority figures, should be inherently resilient and capable of managing any challenge without external support. Such misconceptions silence discussions about educators' emotional struggles, leaving them isolated and without resources to cope effectively.

Additionally, the book highlights the effects of negative and conflictual teacher-student relationships, which can lead to emotional distress in students, including fear, humiliation, and a diminished sense of self-worth. Although teacher-student interactions are widely studied in terms of positive educational outcomes, the detrimental consequences of harmful relational dynamics remain insufficiently explored. Research on the psychological impact of punitive, emotionally distant, or humiliating teaching practices is still limited, despite growing evidence that such experiences shape students' academic engagement, mental health, and self-perception well into adulthood.

Engaging educators, researchers, and policymakers, this book calls for a fundamental revaluation of how we support those who shape future generations. If a single lesson or moment of connection can profoundly impact a student's life, then prioritizing the well-being of educators must be central to building healthier, more sustainable learning environments. By breaking the stigma surrounding teacher mental health, exploring its complexities, and advocating for systemic change, this book seeks to contribute to a more effective educational system, one that enables both teachers and students to grow and succeed within the school environment.

Reference

Recalcati, M. (2014). *L'ora di lezione. Per un'erotica dell'insegnamento. [Class time. For an erotic of teaching]*. Einaudi.

2

Beyond the Blackboard: Exploring the Complexities of Teachers' Mental Health

Abstract Teacher mental health is a multifaceted construct influenced by emotional, cognitive, social, and organizational factors, with significant implications for both educators and the overall school environment. This chapter offers an in-depth examination of the complexities surrounding teacher mental health, highlighting its essential role in promoting professional well-being and maintaining educational quality. It begins by presenting an integrated framework for understanding mental health, followed by an exploration of the risk and protective factors that impact teachers' well-being.

Keywords Teachers' mental health • COVID-19 • Work-related stress • Burnout • Resilience • Social and emotional competencies

2.1 Conceptualizing Mental Health: A Multidimensional Perspective

Mental health is an integral component of overall health, encompassing physical, psychological, and social well-being. Within the fields of educational and developmental psychology, it has been conceptualized through

V. Cavioni, *Fostering Teachers' Mental Health*,
https://doi.org/10.1007/978-3-031-92571-9_2

various theoretical models, each emphasizing distinct dimensions of individual functioning. The diversity of definitions highlights the complexity and multidimensionality of mental health, necessitating a holistic perspective that integrates emotional, cognitive, and social dimensions alongside environmental factors (Cavioni et al., 2020).

Different frameworks have been developed to define mental health. One widely recognized model is Keyes' (2002) three-factor model of well-being, which differentiates between *emotional well-being*, *psychological well-being*, and *social well-being*. Emotional well-being refers to the presence of positive affect, life satisfaction, and an overall sense of happiness, aligning with the hedonic perspective of well-being that prioritizes pleasure and the minimization of distress. This dimension is often assessed through indicators such as positive emotions, subjective life satisfaction, and the absence of negative affect. Psychological well-being, on the other hand, is rooted in the eudaimonic perspective, which views well-being as the realization of human potential. It encompasses self-acceptance, autonomy, personal growth, environmental mastery, and a sense of purpose in life. Individuals with high psychological well-being demonstrate resilience, adaptability, and a strong sense of motivation, facilitating engagement in meaningful activities and goal-directed behaviours. Social well-being reflects an individual's sense of integration and connectedness within their community and broader social networks. This dimension includes five components: social integration (feeling part of a community), social acceptance (holding positive views about others), social contribution (perceiving oneself as a valuable member of society), social actualization (believing in the positive evolution of society), and social coherence (viewing society as comprehensible and structured). This model has been extensively validated across different cultural contexts and is instrumental in understanding the continuum of mental health, ranging from flourishing to languishing (Petrillo et al., 2015).

Additionally, from a psychological perspective, health has been analysed through the framework developed by Stamate et al. (2015), who define it as encompassing two primary poles: *psychological well-being*, which signifies a state of mental health and balance, and *psychological distress*, which reflects the presence of mental health challenges or difficulties. This model further identifies three core dimensions of psychological health: self, others, and work. The "self" dimension includes internal resources such as emotional regulation, resilience, and intrinsic motivation, all of which are essential for maintaining psychological well-being. Individuals who experience coherence between their personal values and professional roles report a stronger sense of fulfilment and vitality, reducing their susceptibility to burnout and stress. The "others" dimension refers to the relational aspects of psychological health, encompassing interactions with family, friends and colleagues. Strong social connections serve as protective factors, fostering emotional support, reducing stress, and enhancing problem-solving capacities. Conversely, strained relationships, lack of social support, and conflicts can contribute to psychological distress, negatively affecting mental well-being. The "work" dimension includes structural and organizational factors that influence an individual's psychological health. Elements such as workload balance, professional autonomy, job security, and institutional support play a crucial role in determining well-being in the workplace. Those who experience support from leadership and colleagues, receive constructive feedback, and have access to professional development opportunities report higher levels of job satisfaction and lower occupational stress. In contrast, excessive workload, ambiguous job expectations, and lack of institutional support can increase the risk of emotional exhaustion and disengagement.

Given the complexity of these perspectives, this book adopts the definition of mental health provided by the World Health Organization (WHO), as it is one of the most widely cited and comprehensive frameworks in the literature. According to the WHO (2005), mental health is a state of well-being in which an individual realizes his or her own abilities, can cope with the normal stresses of life, can work productively, and is able to contribute to his or her community. This definition frames mental health as a dynamic and positive condition, extending beyond the mere absence of mental illness to encompass personal fulfilment, social engagement, and overall psychological well-being. Importantly, mental health should not be perceived as a binary concept in which individuals are either entirely healthy or experiencing psychological illness. Instead, it is best understood as a continuum that spans from optimal well-being—often referred to as flourishing—to moderate mental health, and at its lowest end, languishing. Languishing is characterized by reduced psychological engagement, emotional distress, and impaired functioning.

Viewing mental health as a continuum underscores the need for a proactive approach that extends beyond merely preventing mental illness. Promoting mental health involves implementing actions that create supportive living conditions and environments that foster well-being, enabling individuals, families, and communities to adopt and sustain healthy lifestyles while enhancing emotional functioning and social inclusion (Cavioni et al., 2020). This perspective calls for strategies that not only strengthen individuals' capacity to cope with challenges but also cultivate environments that promote personal and social growth, in the end allowing individuals to flourish.

2.2 Why Teacher Mental Health Matters

Teacher mental health extends beyond individual well-being to include broader systemic factors that shape the teaching profession. Within the field of educational psychology, teacher mental health is often examined concerning occupational well-being, which refers to an educator's overall job satisfaction, work engagement, and ability to balance professional and personal responsibilities (Yildirim, 2014). Consequently, teacher mental health is not merely a personal issue but a systemic one with implications for the entire educational community. When teachers experience well-being, they are more likely to remain engaged in their profession, support student learning, and foster a positive classroom environment. However, when their mental health is neglected, the ripple effects extend beyond individual educators, impacting student engagement, school climate, and overall educational quality. Despite its importance, mental health in educational contexts has historically been secondary to academic performance in both research and policy (Cavioni & Grazzani, 2023). Addressing this imbalance requires a shift in perspective, recognizing that sustainable educational outcomes can only be achieved when teacher well-being is prioritized.

This tendency to prioritize academic outcomes overlooks the foundational importance of mental health within the learning environment

(Weare, 2010). Yet, over a century ago, the importance of mental health in schools was recognized, as seen in a 1906 article in the Journal of the American Medical Association, entitled "Mental Health of School Children" (Anonymous, 1906). This article underscored the pressing need for attention to student mental health, particularly the psychological strain induced by academic pressures. The author noted: "As the end of the school year approached, the newspapers brought the usual crop of sad stories with regard to children on whose developing mental faculties the pressure of school labor had worked serious havoc. [...] There is no doubt that there is a large germ of truth in most of the stories and that, unfortunately, there is every year during June an increased number of reported developments of mental disturbance in children because of the burden of schoolwork placed on them at this time. [...] There seems no doubt that it will eventually be necessary to instruct the teachers as to the initial symptoms that are displayed in the commoner mental disturbances of children in order that the strain of study may be then at once interrupted. This is a work that in its far-reaching benevolence will appeal to all who are interested in making child life more happy and less amenable to the stresses of modern civilization. No effort can seem too great, no warning exaggerated that concerns school children under such circumstances, since it is evident their future careers and life usefulness are at stake" (Anonymous, 1906, p. 40).

This early recognition framed mental health as an aspect of school life heavily influenced by academic pressures, identifying teachers as key figures in recognizing students' psychological distress. The primary focus was on training teachers to observe and identify signs of mental difficulties and advocating for professional development to support student mental health. However, this view limited the role of teachers to that of observers, rather than as individuals whose own mental health significantly impacts their capacity to foster positive outcomes in students.

The current approach to school well-being requires a fundamental reconsideration. For too long, interventions have focused primarily on students, neglecting the crucial role of teachers' mental health in fostering a supportive learning environment. Teachers are key figures in students' socialization, shaping their emotional development through daily interactions. Their ability to regulate emotions and model effective coping strategies significantly influences students' emotional and social competencies (Denham et al., 2014; Ornaghi et al., 2022). The emotional climate of the classroom is also deeply connected to teachers' well-being. Educators who exhibit calmness, patience, and enthusiasm foster positive emotional development in students, reinforcing constructive emotional regulation and social interactions. In contrast, expressions of frustration, anger, or emotional distress can contribute to student dysregulation, impeding their ability to manage emotions effectively. The way teachers respond to students' emotional expressions further shapes their capacity to navigate challenging situations. When teachers validate students' emotions, offer support, and demonstrate constructive emotional regulation, they foster a learning environment that enhances emotional competence. One effective approach, known as emotion coaching, involves directly teaching students about emotions, their underlying causes, and appropriate regulation strategies. This helps students develop emotional awareness and integrate their understanding of emotions into their social interactions (Cefai & Cavioni, 2014).

Teachers' mental health remains a largely stigmatized issue, with one of the primary barriers to addressing it being the persistent misconception that discussions about mental health are synonymous with psychopathology. This outdated perspective reinforces the belief that acknowledging psychological distress is indicative of personal or professional inadequacy. As a result, many educators hesitate to seek support due to fears of being perceived as weak, incapable, or unfit for their roles. Teachers who openly discuss their struggles often risk professional and social consequences, contributing to a culture in which psychological difficulties are suppressed rather than addressed. A fundamental contributor to this stigma is the unrealistic expectation that teachers should consistently embody resilience, motivation, and enthusiasm, maintaining a positive emotional front for students, parents, and colleagues (Hakanen et al., 2006). This unspoken expectation often disregards the complex emotional experiences of educators, reinforcing the idea that they must always appear enthusiastic, dedicated, and emotionally composed, regardless of the challenges they face. Such pressures contribute to a culture of silence surrounding teacher mental health, making it difficult for educators to openly acknowledge and address their emotions in constructive ways.

This mismatch between outward expressions and internal emotional states can result in emotional dissonance, which not only heightens stress and emotional exhaustion but also compromises long-term well-being, increasing the risk of burnout and disengagement (Jennings, 2020).

Educators experiencing psychological distress may often adopt emotional suppression as a coping strategy, consciously inhibiting the expression of their true emotions to meet professional expectations. This form of emotional labour allows teachers to maintain a composed and authoritative presence in the classroom, yet it comes at a psychological cost. Research indicates that chronic emotional suppression is linked to increased stress, emotional exhaustion, and decreased psychological well-being, in due course heightening the risk of burnout and disengagement (Gross & John, 2003). By prioritizing professional performance over their own emotional needs, teachers may inadvertently exacerbate their distress, as suppressing emotions does not eliminate negative feelings but rather intensifies physiological and psychological strain over time (Chang, 2009). Over time, this lack of acknowledgement and systemic support exacerbates occupational stress, reducing job satisfaction and diminishing the quality of student-teacher interactions.

Addressing teacher mental health should not be framed solely as an intervention for those in crisis but as a proactive strategy that enhances the well-being of educators, students, and the broader school community. Mental health exists on a continuum, rather than as a binary state of well-being or pathology (Keyes, 2002). Acknowledging this continuum challenges the outdated belief that addressing mental health implies dysfunction. Instead, it emphasizes psychological well-being as a fundamental element of professional growth. Adopting this perspective requires systemic changes in educational policies, workplace culture, and teacher training to integrate mental health support as a standard and destigmatized component of the profession.

An effective school mental health approach must place teacher well-being at the core of educational policy and practice. Addressing student well-being without considering the psychological health of teachers results in fragmented and unsustainable interventions. However, the prevailing system often regards educators solely as facilitators of instruction, overlooking the profound impact of their mental health on classroom dynamics and student development. Mentally healthy teachers are better equipped to foster strong connections with students, model effective emotional regulation, and cultivate a positive school climate that promotes resilience and academic success (Cavioni et al., 2023a). Conversely, when educators face chronic stress, emotional exhaustion, or dissatisfaction with their work, their ability to establish supportive relationships, create a nurturing learning environment, and respond effectively to students' emotional and academic needs becomes severely impaired (Schonert-Reichl et al., 2017). Thus, promoting teacher well-being is not only beneficial for educators themselves but is also fundamental to the broader success of school-based mental health initiatives. A psychologically healthy teaching workforce is essential for creating emotionally supportive classrooms where students can succeed both academically and personally.

Despite clear evidence of its importance, teacher mental health remains largely overlooked in policy frameworks. Policymakers must recognize that supporting educators' psychological well-being is not an additional concern but a fundamental requirement for a sustainable education system. While significant resources are allocated to student-centred interventions, systemic initiatives focused on teachers' mental health are notably lacking. Educators are expected to provide both emotional and instructional support, yet they are often left without the necessary resources to manage their own well-being.

Cavioni et al. (2020) propose a theoretical framework for mental health promotion in schools that extends beyond student-centred interventions by placing teachers also at the core of the system (see Fig. 2.1). This model acknowledges the reciprocal influence between student and teacher well-being, recognizing that fostering a mentally healthy school environment requires addressing both groups within an integrated approach. The framework is structured around three fundamental components: fostering *social and emotional learning* (SEL), strengthening *resilience*, and preventing *social, emotional, and behavioural difficulties*. Box 2.1 provides a detailed examination of the three components of the model.

Box 2.1 The Three Key Components of the School Mental Health Theoretical Framework

According to the Collaborative for Academic, Social, and Emotional Learning (CASEL), SEL is the process through which individuals acquire and apply knowledge, skills, and attitudes to develop healthy identities, manage emotions, achieve personal and collective goals, demonstrate empathy, establish supportive relationships, and make responsible decisions (Mahoney et al., 2021; Durlak et al., 2024). SEL is a fundamental component of teachers' well-being, as they play a dual role in both managing their own emotional health and fostering these skills in their students. Teachers with well-developed social and emotional competencies are better prepared to navigate the emotional demands of their profession, including managing student behaviours, maintaining a healthy work-life balance, and fostering positive interactions with colleagues and parents (Cavioni et al., 2024). Furthermore, integrating SEL into teachers' professional development enhances classroom management, strengthens teacher-student relationships, and contributes to a more supportive and positive school climate. The second pillar of the framework, resilience, is defined as the capacity to adapt to adversity and recover from challenges (Masten, 2001). Given the high levels of stress, emotional labour, and diverse professional demands inherent in the teaching profession, resilience is particularly critical (Ornaghi et al., 2023). Developing this capacity enables teachers to maintain their well-being while effectively responding to the pressures of their role. The third component of the framework emphasizes the prevention of social, emotional, and behavioural difficulties, which can present in diverse ways among teachers. Educators experiencing such difficulties may exhibit increased irritability, reduced patience in classroom interactions, diminished job satisfaction, and a sense of detachment from both students and colleagues (Hakanen et al., 2006).

Each of these dimensions contributes to the overarching goal of mental health promotion by enhancing protective factors and mitigating risks. Applying a systemic approach, the model accounts for both proximal and distal influences on well-being. It highlights that schools function as complex ecosystems where students, teachers, families, the broader school community and policy-makers interact dynamically. By addressing mental health as an interconnected process rather than an isolated phenomenon, the framework underscores the necessity of school-wide policies and practices that integrate mental health promotion into the educational context. This model calls for a paradigm shift in how mental

Fig. 2.1 School mental health theoretical framework (Cavioni et al., 2020, p. 68)

health is approached in educational settings, moving away from fragmented, student-exclusive initiatives towards an integrated, whole-school strategy that acknowledges the interdependence of teacher and student well-being.

2.3 Understanding Risk and Protective Factors in Teacher Mental Health

Risk and protective factors play a crucial role in shaping teachers' mental health and well-being. Risk factors refer to conditions or characteristics that increase the likelihood of experiencing psychological distress or developing mental health difficulties. These factors can exacerbate stress levels, reduce coping capacity, and contribute to burnout, emotional exhaustion, and overall professional dissatisfaction. In contrast, protective factors are elements that mitigate or counterbalance the negative impact of risk factors, promoting resilience and psychological well-being. These elements enhance teachers' ability to manage professional challenges effectively, sustain motivation, and maintain positive mental health despite workplace stressors.

The following sections examine the risk and protective factors that shape teacher mental health, highlighting their impact on professional sustainability and overall well-being. Key risk factors include work-related stress, post-traumatic stress disorder in educators, teacher burnout, bullying directed at teachers, and emotional abuse by school principals, all of which contribute to significant psychological distress. Conversely, this section will also explore protective factors such as resilience and social-emotional competence, which play a crucial role in mitigating stress, fostering well-being, and supporting long-term professional engagement.

2.3.1 Work-Related Stress in Educators

Work-related stress is broadly defined as the body's physiological and psychological response to external demands that require adaptation. Stress emerges in situations that necessitate change, particularly when individuals perceive these demands as overwhelming or as a threat to their physical and mental well-being. The intensity of stress is largely influenced by an individual's perception of their ability to manage these demands, with higher levels of stress occurring when individuals feel they lack the necessary resources to effectively respond (Lazarus & Folkman, 1984).

A key distinction in stress research is between *eustress* and *distress*. Eustress, often described as "positive stress", occurs when an individual perceives a challenge as within their capacity to manage, leading to motivation, focus, and improved performance. In contrast, distress arises when perceived demands exceed personal resources, resulting in feelings of helplessness, anxiety, and an overall negative impact on well-being. Chronic distress can have significant consequences on both physical and mental health, with research linking prolonged exposure to stress to an increased risk of cardiovascular diseases, gastrointestinal disorders, and psychological conditions such as anxiety, depression, panic attacks, and psychosomatic symptoms (Giorgi et al., 2014).

A critical factor in understanding stress lies in the concept of stressors, which are external or internal stimuli that trigger a stress response. Stressors challenge an individual's ability to adapt, eliciting physiological and psychological stress responses. Their impact can range from mild discomfort to severe, chronic health consequences, depending on their nature, intensity, and duration of exposure. Stressors vary widely in severity, encompassing both everyday challenges, such as workload pressures, interpersonal conflicts, and time constraints, and more severe, extraordinary circumstances, including traumatic life events or significant health concerns. The perception of stressors is highly subjective, as individuals appraise and interpret stress-inducing situations differently based on their personal coping resources, past experiences, and psychological resilience. A situation that one person perceives as manageable may feel overwhelming to another, underscoring the role of cognitive appraisal in the stress response.

Stressors can be categorized into acute and chronic types based on their duration and persistence. Acute stressors are short-term and situation-specific, arising from immediate challenges such as meeting tight deadlines, public speaking, or unexpected disruptions. These stressors typically elicit a temporary stress response that subsides once the situation is resolved. In contrast, chronic stressors persist over time, exerting a prolonged impact on psychological and physical well-being. Long-term exposure to conditions such as job insecurity, sustained interpersonal conflicts, or financial strain can contribute to cumulative stress, increasing vulnerability to mental and physical health problems (McEwen, 1998). Persistent stress can lead to fatigue, cognitive difficulties, and heightened susceptibility to cardiovascular and musculoskeletal disorders. Additionally, elevated cortisol levels, commonly linked to chronic stress, have been shown to negatively impact brain regions essential for memory and learning, particularly the hippocampus (Michie & Cockcroft, 1996).

The teaching profession is widely recognized for its high levels of work-related stress, partly due to the complexity and diversity of tasks teachers must manage daily. Teachers are required to operate on multiple levels, each of which entails distinct forms of responsibility and potential stressors. Pedagogically, they must focus on delivering curriculum content, assessing students, and supporting academic growth. Additionally, teachers are responsible for fostering healthy interpersonal relationships with students, providing emotional and social support, and creating a positive classroom atmosphere that facilitates learning. Teachers must also manage relationships within the school community and maintain interactions with families, coordinating between the classroom environment and external contexts like home (Zurlo et al., 2016).

The literature has identified a multitude of stressors that deeply impact the mental health of teachers, who face specific demands in their professional roles that often surpass their adaptive capacities, leading to significant physical and psychological strain. These stressors, arising from various aspects of the educational environment and the expectations placed on teachers, jointly contribute to a high-risk profile for stress-related outcomes among educators. Within the educational context, stressors are multifaceted and stem from *physical, emotional, task-related, tool-related, human resource, role-related, social, career, organizational*, and *traumatic* sources (Cavioni & Grazzani, 2023).

Physical stressors in schools encompass environmental factors such as overcrowded and noisy classrooms, frequent temperature fluctuations, and outdated infrastructure, all of which contribute to physical discomfort and fatigue. Additionally, inadequate lighting, particularly dim or harsh neon lights, has been shown to impair visual focus, further contributing to teachers' physical exhaustion. Extended periods of standing and continuous movement throughout the classroom environment intensify physical strain, often leading to musculoskeletal pain and chronic fatigue over time.

Emotional stressors emerge from affective responses to challenging classroom dynamics, which often evoke frustration, discouragement, or anger. Teachers may feel helpless or demoralized when students underperform academically despite their efforts or when recurrent behavioural issues arise without sufficient institutional support or effective strategies for intervention. Such stressors can undermine teachers' emotional resilience, particularly in cases where they feel isolated in managing these issues, leading to cumulative emotional strain.

Task-related stressors refer to the high workloads and strict time constraints associated with teaching, including both instructional and bureaucratic tasks. Teachers are frequently required to fulfil multiple responsibilities within limited timeframes, balancing curriculum requirements with administrative duties that extend beyond regular school hours, further eroding work-life balance and contributing to burnout. When the demands exceed teachers' perceived capacities, a sense of inadequacy and tension emerges, impacting job satisfaction and psychological well-being.

Tool-related stressors involve the lack of access to adequate educational resources, such as computers, reliable internet, and up-to-date textbooks. Resource scarcity can restrict teachers' ability to deliver high-quality, interactive, and effective lessons, resulting in frustration and added pressure to meet student needs within these limitations. For instance, schools that lack technological tools hinder teachers' capacity to implement engaging and modernized instructional strategies, impacting both teaching quality and student engagement.

Human resource stressors are related to staffing shortages and insufficient training, which directly affect teachers' capacity to address diverse student needs. Schools with inadequate staff numbers relative to student populations create higher workloads for each teacher, leading to increased stress. Additionally, inadequate training for working with students requiring special accommodations or specific support needs places further strain on teachers, who must often adapt without adequate preparation to ensure equitable educational outcomes.

Role-related stressors pertain to the dual educational and welfare responsibilities teachers assume, alongside the broader societal undervaluation of the teaching profession. Teachers are frequently expected to support students' mental and physical health, which can be particularly challenging in complex classroom settings where they may lack the necessary resources or training to manage students' diverse needs. This added weight of responsibility, combined with a perceived lack of societal appreciation for the teaching profession, negatively affects teachers' professional identity and sense of purpose.

Social stressors arise from interactions within the school environment, including challenging relationships with students, families, colleagues, and administrators. Teachers often face stress from managing problematic student behaviour, dealing with uncooperative parents, or navigating difficult dynamics with unsupportive colleagues or school leaders. These interactions can contribute to a hostile or unsupportive work environment, further exacerbating stress and impacting mental health. Instances of psychological or physical intimidation from students, parents, or colleagues add a layer of distress.

Career-related stressors involve limitations in career progression and financial compensation within the teaching profession. Many teachers experience dissatisfaction with low salaries, limited advancement opportunities, and job insecurity, which contribute to high turnover rates and affect long-term commitment to the profession, disrupting continuity in student education and increasing overall teacher stress.

Organizational stressors stem from continuous policy changes, internal evaluations, and professional development expectations within the educational system. Teachers frequently face pressures to meet evolving standards, adapt to new policies, and complete ongoing training, which can create a sense of instability and diminish their perceived control in their roles. Such organizational demands add to the cumulative stress of teaching and can impact their sense of effectiveness and stability within the profession.

Traumatic event stressors relate to the potential for accidents or incidents involving students and staff, which pose an underlying concern for teachers responsible for student safety. The potential for emergencies, including physical accidents and external threats, contributes to persistent stress among teachers, affecting their sense of security and overall well-being in the workplace.

2.3.2 Post-traumatic Stress Disorder in Teachers: The Psychological Consequences of the COVID-19 Pandemic

The COVID-19 pandemic has significantly affected the psychological well-being of educators across the globe, disrupting various dimensions of both their personal and professional lives. Beyond the immediate stress provoked by the sudden transition to remote teaching and rapidly changing instructional demands, many teachers reported increased levels of psychological distress, including anxiety, emotional exhaustion, and techno-stress (Westphal et al., 2022). This latter form of stress arises from the intensified dependence on digital technologies, often occurring in contexts where educators lack adequate training, technical support, or access to reliable infrastructure. Manifesting as cognitive overload, frustration, and a diminished sense of competence in navigating online platforms, techno-stress has further amplified emotional strain and contributed to a decline in overall well-being (Zheng et al., 2022).

The sudden and prolonged transition to online education, compounded by increased workload, diminished work-life boundaries, and fears of infection contributed to a constellation of stress responses that, in some cases, resembled trauma-related symptomatology. Teachers not only had to manage unfamiliar digital platforms and maintain instructional quality under pressure but also served as emotional anchors for students and families coping with illness, loss, and social isolation. This cumulative burden has underscored the vulnerability of educators to severe psychological outcomes, including symptoms consistent with post-traumatic stress disorder (PTSD), especially in contexts of prolonged uncertainty and limited coping resources. The following section explores the diagnostic framework of PTSD and its relevance to the experiences of teachers during the COVID-19 crisis, with particular attention to empirical findings on pandemic-related trauma exposure in educational settings.

According to the Diagnostic and Statistical Manual of Mental Disorders—DSM-5-TR (APA, 2022), post-traumatic stress disorder.is a psychiatric condition that can develop following exposure to a traumatic event involving actual or threatened death, serious injury, or sexual violence. This exposure may occur through direct personal experience of the traumatic event, witnessing it firsthand as it happens to others, or learning that a close family member or friend has been affected. In cases where the traumatic event involves the actual or threatened death of a loved one, the incident must have been violent or accidental. Additionally, PTSD can arise from repeated or extreme exposure to distressing details of traumatic events, as seen in professionals such as first responders handling human remains or law enforcement officers frequently encountering cases of child abuse. PTSD is marked by intrusions, avoidance, negative cognitive and mood changes, and hyperarousal. Intrusions include distressing memories, nightmares, and flashbacks. Avoidance involves efforts to evade trauma-related thoughts, emotions, or reminders. Negative cognitive and mood changes manifest as distorted beliefs, persistent negative emotions (e.g., fear, guilt, shame), and loss of interest in activities. Hyperarousal symptoms include irritability, hypervigilance, exaggerated startle responses, concentration difficulties, and sleep disturbances. Symptoms last over a month, causing significant distress or impairment. In some cases, dissociative symptoms like depersonalization (feeling detached from oneself) and derealization (perceiving the world as unreal) further intensify PTSD severity.

The COVID-19 pandemic represented one of the most significant global crises in recent history, profoundly affecting mental health on a widespread scale (Gavin et al., 2020). Its psychological toll has been both immediate and enduring, as individuals and societies have navigated the uncertainty, disruption, and instability brought by the virus. Research has documented a sharp rise in psychological distress, with the mental health consequences expected to persist long after the physical health crisis subsides (Gavin et al., 2021). Key contributing factors include prolonged social isolation, fear of contagion, financial insecurity, and the disruption of daily routines, all of which have led to heightened levels of anxiety, depression, and stress-related disorders across various populations (Escobar Lux et al., 2023).

The education sector has been among the hardest hit, as schools were among the first institutions forced to undergo significant changes. Teachers faced exceptional psychological challenges due to their professional responsibilities and the sudden shift in instructional delivery. Studies conducted during the pandemic suggest that educators were especially vulnerable to symptoms of PTSD, as they struggled to adapt to unprecedented demands while managing their own well-being. Meta-analytical data indicate that 11% of teachers reported PTSD symptoms, with significant variability across different regions and educational levels (Idoiaga Mondragon et al., 2023). The abrupt transition to remote teaching, prolonged working hours, frequent modifications to health and safety protocols, and inadequate preparation for online instruction led to occupational stress, emotional exhaustion, and burnout. Additionally, the social isolation of both teachers and students further exacerbated these stressors, creating a learning environment marked by uncertainty and disengagement.

While most schools remained closed, in some countries, certain teachers, particularly those in leadership roles or special education teachers, continued working in highly stressful conditions. Due to the need for ongoing support for students with special educational needs, these educators were required to physically remain in schools, often working in empty classrooms with only a few students present. To prevent virus transmission, they had to maintain strict hygiene measures, further adding to the complexity of their work environment. Many of these teachers reported experiencing intense anxiety and fear of infection, compounded by the emotional strain of working in near-isolation while most of their colleagues and students remained at home under government-imposed lockdowns. As educators transitioned back to in-person teaching, the lingering threat of viral infection heightened their psychological distress. Given the inherently interactive nature of teaching, social distancing measures disrupted traditional classroom dynamics, making it particularly challenging to foster meaningful engagement with younger students. Moreover, teachers served as key emotional support figures for students and their families, many of whom were coping with illness, loss, financial insecurity, and prolonged isolation (Fan et al., 2021).

Lastly, teachers who had been diagnosed with COVID-19 or had lost close family members to the virus exhibited a substantially higher prevalence of PTSD symptoms, reinforcing the association between direct trauma exposure and psychological distress. The most frequently reported symptoms included intrusive thoughts, sleep disturbances, emotional dysregulation, and cognitive impairments (Fan et al., 2021).

2.3.3 Teacher Burnout: The Toll of Exhaustion in Schools

Burnout, also referred to as "burnout syndrome" due to its complex and multifactorial nature, is a pathological condition that arises from prolonged exposure to occupational stress. It is particularly prevalent in high-emotion professions, especially within the helping sectors, where initially acute stressors evolve into chronic strain. According to the multidimensional theory of burnout (Maslach, 1982; Maslach et al., 2001), the syndrome is characterized by three core dimensions: emotional exhaustion, a sense of cynicism, and a perceived decline in personal efficacy or accomplishment.

Exhaustion is the most reported component of burnout and represents its core individual stress dimension. It is characterized by a profound sense of fatigue that permeates physical, emotional, and cognitive functioning. Individuals experiencing exhaustion often report difficulties with concentration, sleep disturbances, and a range of physical symptoms, such as gastrointestinal issues, headaches, and excessive sweating - signs of somatization linked to prolonged stress exposure. This state reflects the cumulative toll of sustained effort in response to demanding work conditions, leading to a reduction of energy reserves and a decline in overall functioning and performance capacity. *Cynicism* reflects the interpersonal dimension of burnout and involves a negative, emotionally detached attitude towards one's work and the people associated with it. It is characterized by a sense of indifference, callousness, or disengagement, often manifesting as a loss of empathy and a diminished sense of connection with colleagues or students. Individuals experiencing cynicism may withdraw from social interactions, disregard others' needs, or display dismissive and distancing behaviours. This emotional disengagement often functions as a psychological defence mechanism against excessive emotional demands; however, it can severely undermine interpersonal relationships and contribute to a dysfunctional or unsupportive work environment. The *sense of ineffectiveness*, also referred to as reduced personal accomplishment, represents the self-evaluative dimension of burnout. It involves persistent feelings of inadequacy, diminished professional efficacy, and a perceived lack of achievement in one's work. This component is often marked by self-doubt, decreased motivation, and emotional responses such as frustration, guilt, and anger. Individuals may struggle to recognize the value of their contributions and experience a growing sense of failure in fulfilling their professional roles. In educational settings, this can manifest as uncertainty about one's ability to positively influence student learning and engagement, leading to a loss of purpose and perceived control over work-related demands. Over time, these experiences can foster a self-critical mindset and reinforce the downward spiral associated with burnout (Schwarzer & Hallum, 2008).

Burnout often includes diminished reflective capacity, where individuals struggle to view their work experiences with perspective and balance. Work can take on excessive importance, making it difficult to "switch off" mentally and approach challenges with objectivity. This over-identification with work blurs the boundary between professional and personal life, leading to difficulty in disengaging from work-related thoughts and stressors, even outside of work hours. This loss of objectivity perpetuates stress by entrenching individuals further into their professional roles at the expense of their overall well-being (Bakker & Demerouti, 2007).

In clinical settings, burnout syndrome is approached differently within various diagnostic frameworks. While the DSM-5-TR (the Diagnostic and Statistical Manual of Mental Disorders, Fifth Edition Text Revision) does not classify burnout as a distinct mental disorder, it includes a section entitled "Cultural concepts of distress" that discusses cultural expressions, and perceptions related to distress. Such a section provides insight into how individuals from various cultural backgrounds interpret and communicate experiences of suffering, including idioms and phrases commonly used in the U.S., such as "burnout", "feeling stressed", "nervous breakdown", and "feeling depressed". These terms act as cultural expressions of distress, allowing individuals to communicate a range of discomfort or dissatisfaction without necessarily meeting the formal criteria for a psychiatric disorder. In this framework, "burnout" serves as a socially recognized term that captures common psychological reactions to workplace stress. It reflects a shared cultural understanding of exhaustion and disillusionment tied to work yet does not imply a clinically diagnosed condition. Rather, it is a way for individuals to describe a relatable experience of stress and fatigue within a professional context. In contrast, the International Classification of Diseases, 11th Revision (ICD-11) by the World Health Organization classifies burnout specifically as an occupational phenomenon, recognizing it as a condition linked to chronic, unmanaged workplace stress, though it is not defined as a medical disorder. More specifically, the ICD-11 categorizes burnout within the chapter titled "Factors influencing health status or contact with health services", which includes reasons for seeking medical care that are not classified as diseases or health conditions. The ICD-11 defines burnout as an occupational syndrome characterized by three primary dimensions: persistent feelings of energy depletion or exhaustion, a growing mental detachment from one's job often accompanied by negative or cynical attitudes towards work and a diminished sense of professional efficacy. This classification distinctly situates burnout within the occupational context, emphasizing that the term should not be extended to encompass stressors or challenges encountered outside of work. Unlike the DSM-5-TR, which regards burnout as a cultural idiom of distress without formal diagnostic status, the ICD-11 conceptualizes burnout as a work-related syndrome deserving of attention within healthcare as a distinct condition tied specifically to workplace stress, rather than a general health disorder.

Within educational settings, teachers experiencing burnout may struggle significantly with routine classroom management, such as maintaining order or engaging students in lesson activities. Symptoms may include anxiety, panic attacks,[1] disengagement, and a lack of empathy, with some educators exhibiting disdain towards students and colleagues and occasionally resorting to offensive or derogatory language. Burnout in educators is associated with multiple risk factors, which include personal, relational, organizational, and sociocultural dimensions (Avanzi et al., 2013). Table 2.1 describes the risk factors associated with teacher burnout.

The societal implications of teacher stress and burnout are far-reaching, affecting not only the well-being of individual educators and the school context, but also generating significant costs associated with absenteeism, reduced productivity, high turnover rates, and premature retirement. Prolonged psychological distress can lead teachers to take extended sick leave or, in severe cases, request work disability due to occupational illness, further exacerbating the shortage of qualified educators and impacting overall educational quality (Bakker & Demerouti, 2007; Cavioni & Grazzani, 2023).

---

[1] Panic attacks are sudden episodes of overwhelming fear or acute distress that peak within minutes and are accompanied by a range of physical and/or cognitive symptoms. They can be expected, occurring in response to a known trigger or feared situation, or unexpected, emerging spontaneously without an identifiable cause (APA, 2022).

Table 2.1 Factors contributing to teacher burnout (adapted from Cavioni & Grazzani, 2023)

Factor	Description
Personal	Include individual characteristics such as personality traits, age, professional expectations, resilience, emotional regulation abilities, coping skills, and one's sense of control over events. Teachers' lifestyles, family circumstances, and cognitive styles also influence how they experience and manage stress. For example, educators with strong emotional regulation skills and effective coping strategies may be better equipped to handle the daily pressures of the teaching profession, thereby reducing their risk of burnout. In contrast, those with a lower sense of control or less effective coping mechanisms may feel overwhelmed, leading to heightened vulnerability to stress and exhaustion
Relational	It refers to the quality of social interactions with colleagues, school administrators, non-teaching staff, students, and students' families. Positive, supportive relationships with these groups can provide a buffer against burnout, fostering a sense of belonging and professional support. However, strained or unsupportive interactions, such as conflicts with colleagues or difficult relationships with parents, can amplify stress and contribute to a sense of isolation and professional dissatisfaction
Organizational	It encompasses elements related to the structure and conditions of the work environment, including the availability of teaching resources, the management of meetings, role assignments, and workload distribution. Work environments with inadequate resources, excessive administrative demands, or poorly defined roles can create high levels of stress, undermining teachers' sense of efficacy and control. An environment that fosters collaboration and offers adequate resources, however, can enhance job satisfaction and reduce the risk of burnout.
Sociocultural	It pertains to aspects of the broader educational and community context in which teachers work. Schools characterized by high levels of academic failure, dropout rates, and limited resources may lead teachers to experience distrust, dissatisfaction, demotivation, and stress. In contrast, schools characterized by high-achieving students, ample resources, and a strong culture of academic excellence tend to foster greater job satisfaction and professional self-efficacy among teachers which is the confidence in their ability to positively impact on student learning. Sociocultural factors also include recent shifts in educational policy and practice

2.3.4 Under Attack: Bullying Against Teachers

Bullying has traditionally been conceptualized as a peer-to-peer phenomenon, with early research focusing on student-on-student aggression. Pioneering studies by Olweus (1994) provided the foundational framework for understanding school bullying, defining it as a form of aggressive behaviour that is intentional, repeated over time, and occurs within an interpersonal relationship characterized by an imbalance of power. Bullying consists of negative actions that can be perpetrated or experienced by one or more individuals. These actions involve the intentional infliction or attempted infliction of harm or discomfort to others. This framework was instrumental in shaping anti-bullying policies and interventions worldwide, focusing primarily on protecting students from victimization within the school environment (Downes & Cefai, 2016; Murphy, 2024; UNESCO, 2024; Zanetti & Caravita, 2018).

Research has increasingly acknowledged that bullying in educational settings is not limited to student-to-student interactions (Burns et al., 2020). Teachers are also becoming targets, with bullying often perpetrated by students and, in some cases, by parents or even school administrators (Kauppi & Pörhölä, 2012; Terry, 1998). This shift in focus highlights that bullying extends beyond peer interactions, emerging as a widespread systemic issue that impacts the entire school environment. Despite its significant implications, it remains an underexplored and often overlooked phenomenon, likely due to its sensitive and complex nature.

Bullying directed at teachers is often referred to as teacher-targeted bullying (TTB). Matsui (2005) defines TTB as including threats of physical assault, verbal abuse, racial and sexual slurs, repeated intimidation, disrespectful behaviour, vandalism of personal belongings, and persistent class disruption. Like student bullying, TTB is intentional, repetitive, and aims to harm the victim physically, emotionally, socially, and/or professionally. The forms of aggression involved can be verbal (e.g., insults, threats), non-verbal (e.g., exclusion, passive-aggressive behaviours), physical (e.g., damage to personal belongings, direct assault), sexual (e.g., inappropriate comments, harassment), racial (e.g., discriminatory remarks), and electronic (e.g., cyberbullying through social media or messaging platforms). TTB can be understood along a continuum of severity, ranging from low-level disruptive behaviours to more extreme forms of harassment and violence. The psychological and professional consequences of such aggression are significant, with studies indicating increased levels of stress, emotional exhaustion, job dissatisfaction, and even attrition among teachers who experience sustained victimization. Approximately two-thirds of teachers reported experiencing insulting behaviour, while just under one-third faced harassment, including property vandalism and breaches of their domestic privacy. Furthermore, one in four teachers had been threatened with violence, around 10% had been physically attacked, and a smaller proportion reported incidents of sexual harassment (Salmi & Kivivuori, 2009). Teachers who reported being bullied overwhelmingly identified their aggressors as male students, reinforcing the gendered nature of this form of aggression. Furthermore, these incidents were most frequently carried out by either a single student or a small group of students, rather than by larger peer collectives. This pattern suggests that TTB is often strategic rather than impulsive, with perpetrators seeking to assert dominance and enhance their social standing within the school hierarchy.

The primary motivation behind student-perpetrated bullying against teachers appears to be the pursuit of power and social dominance, with the teacher functioning as a symbolic target in this dynamic. Bullying students often seek to assert control over the classroom by engaging in disruptive behaviours that convey contempt for the teacher, employing coercive tactics intended to undermine the teacher's authority and effectiveness. Rather than being isolated expressions of frustration or dissatisfaction, these behaviours frequently involve acts of defiance, humiliation, and intimidation, allowing perpetrators to elevate their perceived status among peers. Research suggests that students who bully teachers are also likely to engage in peer-directed bullying, indicating that aggression is not merely a situational reaction but a consistent behavioural pattern across different social contexts (Kauppi & Pörhölä, 2012).

While research on teacher-targeted bullying has largely focused on educators as a collective group, recent studies have highlighted that male teachers, despite traditional gender norms positioning them as authoritative figures, are also vulnerable to victimization. A growing body of evidence suggests that assumptions regarding male teachers' resilience may lead to their experiences of bullying being overlooked or minimized (Burns et al., 2024). Box 2.2 explores the phenomenon of male teachers as victims of bullying, challenging common misconceptions about masculinity and authority in the school environment.

The qualitative study conducted by De Wet (2010) provides a comprehensive account of TTB on the nature and severity of the mistreatment that teachers experience at the hands of students. The findings reveal that bullying against teachers manifests in various forms, including verbal,

Box 2.2 Masculinity and Vulnerability: When Male Teachers Face Bullying

The public discourse surrounding masculinity and teaching reinforces the idea that male educators, under their gender, are less likely to experience victimization compared to their female counterparts. This assumption stems from gendered expectations that portray men as assertive, authoritative, and capable of maintaining discipline, thereby making it less socially acceptable, or even conceivable, to view them as targets of bullying. However, empirical studies challenge this perception, demonstrating that male teachers are not immune to student aggression and classroom victimization. Testimonies from male teachers provide compelling evidence that they, too, are subjected to acts of intimidation, disrespect, and professional undermining. Some report experiencing verbal humiliation, threats, and intentional defiance from students, often feeling powerless to respond without reinforcing negative stereotypes of male aggression (Burns et al., 2024). The expectation that male teachers should naturally command respect and control can, paradoxically, leave them particularly vulnerable when they encounter bullying, as seeking support or acknowledging victimization may be perceived as a failure to embody traditional masculine traits.

This intersection between gender norms and teacher victimization has significant psychological and professional implications. Male teachers who experience bullying may face increased stress, emotional distress, and professional burnout, compounded by a reluctance to seek help due to fears of stigma or diminished credibility. The assumption that men are less susceptible to bullying within educational settings not only overlooks their lived experiences but also contributes to the invisibility of their struggles, preventing the development of targeted interventions and support systems. Addressing male teachers' experiences of bullying requires a shift in the educational and psychological discourse surrounding power, authority, and victimization in schools.

non-verbal, emotional, and physical abuse, with incidents occurring both during and outside school hours. One of the most reported forms of bullying was verbal and non-verbal abuse, which included insults, swearing, and ridicule aimed at undermining teachers' authority and dignity. Teachers described how students openly mocked them, refused to comply with instructions, and engaged in acts of public defiance designed to elicit frustration. One participant shared an instance where a student refused to pick up a water bottle when ordered, instead turning his back and walking away, signalling blatant disregard for the teacher's authority. Another teacher recounted, "They do their utmost to ridicule me and if I lose my temper, they laugh at me." Such experiences illustrate the intentional nature of these behaviours, where students actively seek to provoke emotional reactions from educators, exploiting their professional vulnerability.

Beyond verbal harassment, emotional and psychological abuse was another pervasive form of mistreatment. Teachers described being subjected to ongoing intimidation, often involving public humiliation and classroom disruptions. A teacher described how a group of students made his life "*a living hell*" by constantly disrupting lessons, chatting amongst themselves, back-chatting, and openly ignoring him. Such behaviour is not only a direct attack on the teacher's authority but also an attempt to strip them of their professional legitimacy. The psychological toll of these repeated acts of disrespect and insubordination contributes to feelings of powerlessness, emotional exhaustion, and professional disillusionment.

More severe forms of TTB included threats of violence and physical aggression, with some teachers experiencing direct attacks. Participants reported incidents in which students threatened to stab them, shoot them, or cause them physical harm, leading to an overwhelming sense of fear. One educator stated, "I feared for my life." Others described being physically assaulted, with objects thrown at them, being slapped in the face or even chased around the school building. Some principals who participated in the study recounted extreme cases of aggression, with one principal detailing how they were forcibly held captive in their office, their hands tied behind their back, and another being threatened with the murder of their child should they not comply with student demands. The abuse extended beyond the school grounds, as many teachers experienced targeted harassment outside of work. Participants reported students waiting for them in the streets, throwing stones and eggs at their homes, vandalizing their personal property, and spray-painting threatening messages. One teacher recalled, "They waited for me at street corners, armed with stones. They threatened me and said I should watch my back." The premeditated nature of these attacks demonstrates how TTB is not simply a reactionary behaviour but an orchestrated effort to assert dominance over educators and intimidate them both personally and professionally. Some students openly defied and mocked teachers, asserting dominance publicly, while others engaged in anonymous vandalism, damaging classrooms, cars, and personal belongings. These hidden forms of bullying highlight the systematic and calculated nature of TTB, making it harder for teachers to identify perpetrators or seek justice. More than an interpersonal conflict, TTB is a systemic issue that disrupts the entire school environment.

One of the most profound consequences of TTB is the emotional and psychological toll on teachers, leading to chronic stress, burnout, anxiety, and loss of professional confidence. The repeated exposure to verbal abuse, intimidation, and physical threats fosters a state of emotional exhaustion, making it increasingly difficult for teachers to engage effectively with their students. Over time, many educators adopt avoidant behaviours, refraining from disciplinary action or actively disengaging from classroom management to prevent further victimization. This erosion of authority not only compromises their ability to maintain order but also diminishes their sense of self-efficacy as educators, contributing to high attrition rates and early retirements.

Beyond the individual level, TTB has detrimental effects on the broader school environment, leading to a decline in teaching quality and disruptions in classroom dynamics. Educators who feel unsafe or unsupported may adopt passive teaching strategies, minimizing interactions with students to avoid confrontations. This results in lower academic engagement, decreased instructional effectiveness and diminished enthusiasm for teaching. In some cases, teachers may resort to punitive measures, reacting emotionally to student misbehaviour rather than implementing constructive disciplinary practices. The deterioration of teacher-student relationships further exacerbates disciplinary challenges, creating a cycle of hostility and defiance that undermines the overall learning experience (Orange, 2018). Collegiality among staff is also severely affected, as teachers facing bullying often feel isolated and unsupported. A lack of solidarity among colleagues blamed for the victimization, and perceived failures in handling student behaviour contribute to workplace tensions and professional alienation. Some educators may criticize their peers for being too strict or ineffective in managing classroom discipline, while others avoid involvement due to fear of retaliation. This fragmentation within the teaching staff weakens collaborative efforts, discourages open discussions about teacher safety, and reduces opportunities for collective problem-solving. Additionally, school administrators often fail to provide adequate institutional support, sometimes penalizing teachers for their responses to student aggression rather than addressing the root causes of the problem (Andres et al., 2023).

The disruption of school-home relationships is another significant consequence of TTB, as parental involvement in cases of bullying often exacerbates tensions rather than resolves them. Some students use their parents as intermediaries to challenge disciplinary actions, filing complaints against teachers or pressuring school leaders to act in their favour. In extreme cases, gang affiliations within the broader community spill over into the school environment, reinforcing patterns of intimidation against educators. These external influences further destabilize the school climate, making it difficult for teachers to establish respectful and professional relationships with both students and parents. When educators feel unsupported by school leadership and the community, their capacity to enforce rules, maintain discipline, and create a safe learning environment is significantly compromised.

Teacher testimonies underscore the urgent need for schools to recognize, address, and prevent educator victimization through proactive measures. Traditional anti-bullying programmes fail to tackle the power dynamics and professional risks of TTB, leading to erosion of trust, strained teacher-student relationships, and school instability. Without intervention, TTB fosters persistent aggression, psychological distress, and burnout, ultimately compromising education quality. Effective solutions require institutional accountability, strong teacher support, and school-wide prevention strategies, with policies recognizing TTB as a serious occupational hazard through clear reporting procedures and protective measures.

2.3.5 Power and Fear: Teachers Facing Principal Emotional Abuse

The school principal holds a central role in shaping the educational environment, ensuring institutional stability, and fostering a positive and productive school climate. As the primary leader within the school, the principal is responsible for implementing educational policies, guiding teachers and staff, and creating conditions that support student learning and development. This leadership position is grounded in formal authority, derived from institutional policies and administrative responsibilities. However, effective school leadership goes beyond formal authority and relies on social influence - which refers to the ability to motivate, inspire, and guide members of the school community through strong interpersonal relationships - effective communication, and professional expertise. These aspects allow school principals to build trust, encourage collaboration, and shape attitudes and behaviours within the school, fostering a sense of shared vision and collective responsibility among school staff. When formal authority is exercised in conjunction with ethical principles and social and emotional skills, principals can cultivate a culture of respect, collaboration, and shared educational goals. Nevertheless, the possession of power within hierarchical structures inherently carries the risk of misuse or abuse, particularly when leaders lack the necessary competencies to manage authority responsibly. When principals misuse their authority, whether intentionally or inadvertently, this can result in harmful interactions that undermine teachers' well-being and job satisfaction, ultimately affecting the overall school climate.

Keashly (1998) conceptualized emotional abuse as a pattern of hostile verbal and nonverbal behaviours used to exert control over others, often manifesting in intimidation, manipulation, and psychological coercion. In the school setting, when principals misuse their authority, whether intentionally or inadvertently, this can create a toxic work environment, negatively impacting teachers' psychological well-being, job satisfaction, and overall professional performance. Unethical or emotionally abusive leadership can undermine teacher morale, increase stress and burnout, and ultimately hinder the effectiveness of the educational system. Unlike isolated incidents of conflict, emotional abuse in professional settings is characterized by repeated and unwanted behaviours that violate social norms, undermine individual rights, and are perceived as harmful by the target. Individuals are more likely to perceive a superior's behaviour as abusive when it demonstrates a sustained pattern rather than a single occurrence, involves intentional harm, and takes place within a power-imbalanced relationship, where the target has limited ability to resist or retaliate.

In educational contexts, emotional abuse by school administrators towards teachers may manifest through persistent criticism, public humiliation, social exclusion, excessive surveillance, or the intentional withholding of resources and support. These behaviours not only affect the psychological well-being and professional identity of educators but can also have far-reaching implications for teacher effectiveness, job satisfaction, and the overall school climate. Emotional abuse encompasses a range of verbal and nonverbal behaviours that create a hostile, intimidating, or manipulative environment, finally exerting psychological control over the target. Unlike overt physical aggression, emotional abuse operates through persistent and often subtle tactics that undermine an individual's self-worth, professional credibility, and psychological well-being. This form of mistreatment is particularly insidious in hierarchical settings, such as schools, where power imbalances between administrators and teachers may limit the target's ability to resist or seek redress.

Blase and Blase (2002) identify nonverbal manifestations of emotional abuse as including aggressive eye contact, such as staring or giving "dirty looks", as well as social exclusion, such as ignoring or deliberately giving the silent treatment. Additionally, nonverbal abuse can involve intimidating physical gestures, including invading personal space, pointing fingers in an accusatory manner, slamming objects, or even throwing items to express dominance and hostility. These behaviours function as mechanisms of coercion and intimidation, reinforcing the superior's control over the target. Verbal abuse, on the other hand, encompasses a wide spectrum of behaviours designed to demean, belittle, and manipulate the victim. This may include public humiliation, yelling, excessive criticism, name-calling, or angry outbursts, all of which erode professional confidence and self-esteem. Additionally, workplace abusers may engage in gaslighting tactics, such as lying, distorting reality, or dismissing an individual's concerns and emotions, leading to increased stress, self-doubt, and emotional exhaustion. Another common verbal abuse strategy is withholding vital resources or obstructing professional growth opportunities, thereby restricting the target's ability to perform effectively or advance in their career. Further abusive behaviours include favouritism, exclusion, malicious rumour-spreading, and unjustified threats of job loss, all of which contribute to a toxic organizational climate. Stealing credit for another's work, imposing unreasonable job demands, and blaming are also tactics used to create a culture of instability and insecurity within the workplace.

Workplace abuse has widespread and damaging effects, negatively impacting an individual's physical health, psychological well-being, professional performance, and social relationships. The persistent nature of mistreatment contributes to chronic stress, emotional exhaustion, and long-term psychological distress, significantly impairing both personal and occupational functioning. Physically, workplace abuse is closely linked to stress-related ailments, including chronic fatigue, sleep disturbances, headaches, and a weakened immune system, making individuals more susceptible to illness. Prolonged exposure to a toxic work environment can lead to hypertension, heart arrhythmias, ulcers, and irritable bowel syndrome, as sustained stress disrupts physiological regulation. Additionally, weight fluctuations, dermatological issues, and substance abuse are commonly reported, reflecting the connection between workplace mistreatment and maladaptive coping mechanisms. Skin conditions, such as eczema, psoriasis, and stress-induced acne, often arise as a physiological response to chronic stress and heightened cortisol levels, which can trigger inflammation and disrupt the skin barrier (Sun & Rieder, 2021). Furthermore, maladaptive coping mechanisms, which refer to behavioural and psychological strategies that individuals use to manage stress in ineffective or harmful ways (Folkman & Lazarus, 1988), frequently emerge in response to toxic work environments. This includes substance abuse, emotional eating,[2] and social withdrawal, as individuals attempt to alleviate distress through temporary but ultimately counterproductive means. In extreme cases, prolonged exposure to workplace abuse has been associated with suicidal ideation, underscoring the severe risks linked to persistent mistreatment (Pearson et al., 2001). Beyond physical health, workplace abuse has profound psychological consequences, leading to depression, anxiety, and feelings of helplessness and powerlessness, which erode self-confidence and diminish self-worth. Victims often experience anger, cynicism, self-doubt, guilt, and embarrassment, which can escalate to hypervigilance, panic attacks, and, in severe cases, post-traumatic stress disorder (APA, 2022). As a result, many individuals develop deep-seated distrust in professional relationships, further exacerbating emotional withdrawal and disengagement, which, in turn, impairs workplace collaboration and social integration.

Workplace abuse also severely impacts professional functioning, resulting in decreased motivation, job satisfaction, and organizational commitment. Victims often struggle with lower productivity, diminished engagement, and reduced work effort, making it increasingly challenging to perform their tasks effectively. Chronic mistreatment affects cognitive efficiency, concentration, and decision-making abilities, increasing the likelihood of errors, decreased output, and diminished professional engagement. Moreover, toxic work environments are associated with higher absenteeism, increased turnover, and greater job attrition, as individuals seek to escape harmful conditions (Coetzee & van Dyk, 2018). The impact of workplace mistreatment extends beyond the professional domain, affecting an individual's social relationships and overall sense of belonging. Many victims report social withdrawal, isolation, and difficulty maintaining friendships, both within and outside the workplace. Workplace exclusionary tactics, such as rumour-spreading, favouritism, and deliberate social ostracization, further marginalize individuals, fostering a culture of fear and hostility. Over time, persistent mistreatment

[2] Emotional eating refers to the use of food as a means of coping with negative emotions such as stress, anxiety, or frustration, rather than eating in response to physical hunger. This behaviour may provide momentary comfort, but over time, it can contribute to negative physical and psychological consequences, further exacerbating distress (Arnow et al., 1995).

weakens interpersonal trust, reduces emotional support from colleagues, and leads to greater psychological detachment from the workplace community, further exacerbating the emotional toll.

In a qualitative study, Blase and Blase (2006) examined teachers' experiences of emotional abuse and mistreatment by school principals through semi-structured interviews. The study's findings categorized these behaviours into three distinct levels of increasing aggression and severity: (1) *indirect and moderately aggressive*, (2) *direct and escalating aggression*, and (3) *direct and severely aggressive*. These levels represent a continuum of mistreatment, each with differing effects on teachers' psychological health, professional effectiveness, and the overall classroom environment.

At the first level of mistreatment, principals engage in subtle, indirect, and moderately aggressive behaviours that systematically undermine teachers' professional standing and emotional security. This includes ignoring teachers' needs and concerns, refusing to acknowledge personal hardships such as bereavement, and employing stonewalling tactics, deliberately failing to respond to requests or communications. Additionally, principals display favouritism, unfairly denying resources, withholding professional development opportunities, and may take credit for teachers' work. Teachers also reported public reprimands and non-supportive behaviour, particularly in conflicts with students or parents, making them feel isolated and vulnerable in disciplinary situations. Unprofessional conduct, such as engaging in personal affairs or neglecting administrative responsibilities, further exacerbates a climate of disrespect and emotional neglect.

The second level is characterized by direct and intensifying aggression, where principals move from passive neglect to active control and intimidation. This includes spying on teachers by listening in on classes, standing outside classrooms unannounced, or soliciting information from favoured colleagues or parents. The study also documents instances of sabotage, where principals deliberately instruct other staff members to withhold assistance from targeted teachers or disrupt their initiatives. Reports of stealing teachers' personal and professional materials, such as educational resources or equipment, suggest an intentional effort to create an unstable work environment. Additionally, the destruction of instructional materials, such as reading aids, and unreasonable work demands, including forcing teachers to complete the principal's administrative tasks, indicate a pattern of deliberate exploitation. Public and private criticism becomes more severe, often involving humiliation, shouting, and emotional degradation in front of students, colleagues, or parents.

The most extreme category involves direct, severe, and intentionally harmful behaviours that demonstrate a calculated effort to intimidate, threaten, or remove teachers from their positions. Many teachers reported that principals appeared fully aware of their harmful actions and, when confronted, engaged in denial, blame-shifting, and retaliation. This level of mistreatment includes habitual lying, where principals provide false information about teachers' performance, deny support in conflicts, and fabricate accusations against them. Explosive behaviours, including aggressive shouting and physical intimidation, were commonly reported, making the workplace highly volatile. More disturbingly, principals issued direct threats, such as coercing teachers to change student grades or punishing those who expressed dissenting opinions. Teachers were frequently subjected to unwarranted disciplinary actions, including false reprimands, unfair evaluations, and deliberate obstructions to career advancement, such as blocking transfers or issuing negative references. Some principals also engaged in severe ethical violations, including racism, sexual harassment, and even mistreatment of students, particularly targeting vulnerable student populations such as those in special education. This study highlights the long-term impact of principal mistreatment, revealing its detrimental effects on teachers' mental health, job performance, and commitment to the profession. Many educators reported experiencing chronic stress, burnout, and a significant decline in self-confidence, which ultimately led to withdrawal from school-wide initiatives and reduced professional collaboration. The emotional toll of such mistreatment not only undermined their sense of professional identity but also contributed to disengagement from the broader educational community.

The issue of principal mistreatment of teachers is an increasingly recognized concern within educational systems, necessitating comprehensive strategies to prevent harmful leadership behaviours (Cho & Corkett, 2023). Over the past few decades, the role of school principals has undergone significant transformations, expanding far beyond traditional administrative duties to include responsibilities related to school reform, accountability measures, collaborative decision-making, and instructional leadership. While these changes aim to enhance school effectiveness and student outcomes, they have also placed substantial bureaucratic and managerial burdens on principals, leading to a shift in focus from instructional and relational leadership to administrative efficiency. Principals today are required to handle extensive paperwork, budget management, compliance with educational policies, and performance evaluations, often at the expense of building strong, supportive relationships with teachers and fostering a positive school climate. As a result, professional development for school leaders has become heavily oriented towards administrative competencies, with limited training on social and emotional skills related to conflict resolution and ethical leadership. This imbalance can inadvertently contribute to toxic work environments, where principals may, often unintentionally, engage in behaviours that undermine teachers' well-being and job satisfaction due to a lack of awareness about the psychological and emotional impact of leadership decisions.

To address this issue, it is imperative to implement systemic initiatives that provide school leaders with the necessary knowledge and competencies to manage power dynamics constructively and support teachers effectively. One of the most effective leadership models in this context is *ethical leadership*, which, in the case of school principals, is characterized by moral integrity, fairness, and responsibility, shaping decision-making processes and interactions within the school community (Özgenel & Aksu, 2020). Ethical school leaders emphasize transparency, accountability, and the well-being of all stakeholders, ensuring a supportive and equitable educational environment. By serving as role models, they cultivate trust, collaboration, and respect, reinforcing a positive school culture. Ethical leadership has been linked to enhanced organizational outcomes, including higher teacher morale, increased job satisfaction, and a healthier school climate. These factors, in turn, help alleviate stress, burnout, and turnover rates, fostering a more sustainable teaching environment. Effective training programmes should equip principals with the necessary skills to recognize the far-reaching impact of their leadership style on teacher well-being, performance, and mental health. By embracing ethical leadership, school principals can become catalysts for positive change, fostering inclusive and collaborative school environments where teachers feel valued, respected, and motivated to contribute to student success.

2.3.6 Building Strength in Adversity: The Role of Resilience

Resilience is a complex and dynamic construct that has garnered significant attention in psychological research since the late 1970s. Initially conceptualized as an individual's ability to maintain positive functioning despite adversity, this traditional definition has been critiqued for its overemphasis on personal traits while neglecting the broader ecological and systemic influences (Block & Kremen, 1996; Luthar & Zelazo, 2003). A more contemporary understanding, as proposed by Ungar (2018), defines resilience as the capacity to access, negotiate, and utilize health-enhancing resources within one's physical and social environments. This perspective highlights the interactive nature of resilience, emphasizing that it emerges through the interplay of individual attributes (such as self-regulation and coping strategies), supportive relationships (including family, peers, and colleagues), and accessible community resources (such as professional development and institutional support).

Within the context of education, teacher resilience can be understood as an ability, a process, and an outcome and it reflects an educator's capacity to leverage both personal strengths and external resources to effectively manage professional challenges, illustrating the dynamic interplay between individual characteristics and environmental influences (Beltman, 2015; Beltman et al., 2011). Resilient teachers are not merely those who endure adversity but those who actively develop strategies to adapt, thrive, and sustain their motivation over time (Cefai et al., 2021; Höltge et al., 2021).

The following sections explore the protective factors that promote teacher resilience and the risk factors that threaten their well-being. By examining these elements, this discussion aims to highlight the critical role of both individual and contextual resources in supporting educators throughout their careers.

Mansfield et al. (2012) proposed a four-dimensional framework of teacher resilience, highlighting the protective factors that sustain teachers in the profession. This model identifies *emotional*, *motivational*, *professional*, and *social dimensions* as key elements that enhance resilience and promote teacher retention.

The emotional dimension of teacher resilience encompasses the ability to regulate emotions, maintain well-being, and effectively manage the emotional challenges of the profession. Given that teaching is inherently an emotionally demanding role, emotional regulation plays a crucial role in sustaining resilience. Emotionally resilient teachers employ proactive coping strategies, such as problem-solving, seeking support, and reframing setbacks as learning opportunities. They can let go of failures, adapt, and move forward, rather than dwelling on negative experiences. They also prioritize self-care, taking active responsibility for their well-being while maintaining a sense of humour to cope with daily challenges. Their ability to effectively manage job-related stress, maintain emotional stability, and recover quickly from difficulties enhances both their job satisfaction and overall well-being. Teachers with strong emotional regulation skills experience lower levels of burnout and greater professional fulfilment.

The motivational dimension of resilience is defined by optimism, enthusiasm, intrinsic motivation, and perseverance in overcoming challenges, all of which are essential in maintaining teachers' engagement and commitment to their profession. Teachers with high motivational resilience sustain their enthusiasm for teaching, establish realistic expectations and professional goals, and remain persistent in the face of challenges. Those who perceive teaching as an ongoing learning process and proactively seek opportunities for growth and professional development are more likely to stay engaged and committed to the profession. Moreover, self-efficacy is widely recognized as a key determinant of teacher resilience, strengthening their ability to overcome challenges and maintain long-term professional engagement. Resilient teachers demonstrate a strong sense of competence and confidence, drawing motivation from their accomplishments and taking pride in their successes. This sense of efficacy significantly influences their perseverance, tenacity and ability to navigate challenges, reinforcing their capacity to withstand adversity and remain committed to the profession. Notably, efficacy beliefs are most malleable during the early years of teaching, making this period critical for fostering resilience, as once established, these beliefs tend to be more resistant to change (Tait, 2008).

The professional dimension of teacher resilience encompasses the skills, competencies, and practices that enable educators to effectively manage their responsibilities and sustain their professional growth. Teachers who demonstrate professional resilience possess strong instructional skills, set high expectations for student achievement, and are committed to helping students succeed. This dimension is particularly relevant in fostering a sense of self-efficacy and professional competence, both of which are linked to teacher retention (Gu & Day, 2007). They exhibit pedagogical adaptability, confidently applying a diverse range of instructional strategies to meet the needs of their students while fostering engaging and inclusive learning environments. Teachers with high professional resilience demonstrate organizational skills, time management, and proactive engagement in their profession, often taking on roles as mentors, leaders, and role models within their school communities. They are creative and reflective practitioners, continuously refining their teaching methods and striving for improvement. Reflective practice is crucial for professional resilience, allowing teachers to evaluate their experiences, improve teaching methods, and maintain a growth mindset. Additionally, ongoing professional learning plays a critical role in sustaining resilience, as teachers who actively seek professional development opportunities and remain committed to their learning are better equipped to adapt to educational challenges and sustain long-term engagement in the profession.

The social dimension of resilience underscores the significance of collegial relationships, help-seeking behaviours, and effective communication skills. Resilience is not cultivated in isolation but develops through interpersonal connections and social support networks (Cefai et al., 2021). Teachers who actively seek guidance, engage in professional collaboration, and build supportive relationships with colleagues are better prepared to navigate the challenges of their profession. A positive school culture plays a crucial role in fostering these relationships, helping to mitigate stress and reinforce professional commitment. Colleagues provide both emotional and practical support, sustaining morale and strengthening a sense of belonging. However, challenging working conditions, such as excessive workloads, and teacher shortages can weaken collegial bonds, pushing teachers into a state of survival mode that increases stress, burnout, and professional dissatisfaction. Conversely, when schools promote fair workloads and cultivate an atmosphere of trust and collaboration, collegial relationships thrive. In such environments, motivated and optimistic peers can have a positive ripple effect, reinforcing engagement, resilience, and overall well-being in the teaching community.

The ability to establish and maintain these supportive relationships is also influenced by working conditions. Schools that foster a healthy work environment, through structured leadership, fair workload distribution, and equitable resource allocation, create the conditions for meaningful professional interactions. Excessive workloads, a lack of preparation time, and unrealistic expectations can limit teachers' ability to engage in collegial relationships, making them feel isolated and unsupported. Conversely, schools that implement fair class assignments, provide adequate time for lesson planning, and reduce unnecessary administrative burdens allow teachers to dedicate time to collaboration and peer support. Among the most significant sources of support is strong institutional backing from the school administration. When school leadership is structured, transparent, and responsive, teachers are more likely to feel valued and supported. Schools that promote effective leadership, equitable resource distribution, and constructive feedback create environments that foster teacher well-being.

Mentorship is another critical protective factor, particularly for early-career teachers. Having a positive, professional, and prosocial mentor, especially one from the same subject area, significantly enhances teacher retention, self-reflection, and problem-solving skills. However, mentorship programmes can only be effective if they are well structured and properly resourced.

Regarding risk factors, numerous aspects have been identified that weaken teachers' resilience, making them more vulnerable to stress, burnout, and ultimately leaving the profession. Beltman et al. (2011) emphasize that the school and classroom environment plays a pivotal role in shaping teacher resilience, as it can either support or hinder their ability to cope with professional challenges. Challenges within this setting are often directly linked to student behaviour, resource availability, and institutional support structures. One of the most frequently reported difficulties involves *classroom management*, particularly dealing with disruptive students, which places considerable emotional and cognitive strain on teachers. Additionally, teachers often struggle to meet the diverse needs of disadvantaged students, particularly in under-resourced educational settings where additional support mechanisms may be lacking. Moreover, *relationships with students parents* can become a source of tension, especially when conflicts arise over student behaviour, academic expectations, or disciplinary actions. Furthermore, the *absence of adequate mentorship for new educators* can leave them feeling unsupported and ill-equipped to manage classroom challenges effectively. Box 2.3 explored the challenges encountered by early-career teachers, highlighting the risk factors that contribute to high attrition rates.

A significant organizational stressor within schools is *unsupportive or disorganized leadership*. Teachers who perceive their administration as ineffective, inconsistent, or indifferent report higher levels of stress and lower job satisfaction. This challenge is compounded by limited access to

Box 2.3 The Challenges of Early-Career Teachers

Teaching can be often perceived as a vocation rather than a structured profession, a calling driven by intrinsic motivation, a passion for education, and a desire to support students, particularly those students facing difficulties. While this perspective can be inspiring, it also risks reinforcing the misconception that effective teaching relies solely on personal disposition and altruism rather than specialized knowledge and professional competencies. Viewing teaching as a mission rather than a structured career requiring extensive training may contribute to overlooking the necessity of psychological and pedagogical preparation and evidence-based instructional approaches and strategies. The idealized perception of teaching as an innate ability rather than a profession requiring rigorous training can lead to significant disillusionment, particularly among early-career teachers. Many pre-service educators enter the profession expecting to create meaningful change and foster deep student connections, only to grapple with the realities of classroom management, diverse student needs, and institutional constraints (Cavioni et al., 2023b). This discrepancy between expectations and the complex realities of teaching can result in emotional exhaustion, reduced self-efficacy, and ultimately, high attrition rates among new teachers (Mansfield et al., 2016).

Research has shown that the early years of a teaching career are particularly challenging, with studies indicating that 40–50% of new teachers leave the profession within the first five years (Gallant & Riley, 2014; Schaefer, 2013). This pattern has been further confirmed by research analysing specific career trajectories. For example, Miller (2024) found that, on average, 74% of early-career music teachers remained in their positions each year, underscoring the instability of early teaching roles and the variability in retention rates across different subject areas.

teaching materials, equipment, and resources, which hinders instructional effectiveness and increases workload demands.

Social and geographic isolation further exacerbates these difficulties, particularly for teachers working in rural or underserved communities, where access to peer support, mentorship, and professional development opportunities may be limited. Additionally, teachers face scrutiny from multiple stakeholders, including colleagues, parents, and school administrators, leading to pressure to meet external expectations and maintain professional credibility.

Beyond the immediate school environment, teachers must navigate broader systemic challenges that affect their ability to remain engaged and resilient. One of the most prominent issues is excessive *workload* and *time constraints*, which arise from non-teaching responsibilities such as administrative tasks, reporting requirements, and extracurricular duties. Many educators also struggle with difficult courses or classes, where curriculum demands exceed their level of preparation or where student performance expectations create additional pressure. Additionally, *externally imposed regulations*, including standardized testing requirements, policy changes, and bureaucratic oversight, further contribute to teacher stress by limiting instructional autonomy. Job insecurity and poor hiring practices also create instability, particularly for early-career teachers or those in temporary or contract positions.

The financial realities of the teaching profession also play a role in job satisfaction and retention. Low salaries and insufficient school funding contribute to financial stress, making it difficult for teachers to sustain long-term careers in education. Underfunded schools may also lack the necessary resources to support both teachers and students, placing additional burdens on educators who are expected to compensate for systemic deficiencies.

2.3.7 The Importance of Teacher's Social and Emotional Competencies

Historically, Social and Emotional Learning (SEL) has been conceptualized primarily as a framework for fostering students' socio-emotional competencies, equipping them with essential skills to navigate academic, social, and personal challenges. The CASEL framework outlines five core competencies—*self-awareness, self-management, social awareness, relationship skills,* and *responsible decision-making*—which collectively contribute to students' well-being, academic success, and positive life outcomes. Box 2.4 outlines the five core competencies of SEL according to the CASEL framework.

Box 2.4 The SEL Competencies (Mahoney et al., 2021)

- *Self-awareness* refers to the ability to recognize and understand one's emotions, thoughts, and values, as well as their influence on behaviour across different contexts. It involves developing an accurate self-concept, identifying personal strengths and limitations, and fostering a sense of confidence and purpose. Students with strong self-awareness can integrate their personal and social identities, acknowledge their cultural and linguistic assets, and reflect on their emotions to guide their actions.
- *Self-management* encompasses the capacity to regulate emotions, thoughts, and behaviours effectively in various situations to achieve personal and academic goals. It includes self-discipline, stress management, goal-setting, and the ability to delay gratification. Students who demonstrate strong self-management skills exhibit resilience in the face of challenges, maintain motivation to pursue long-term objectives, and adapt successfully to different social and academic demands.
- *Social awareness* is the ability to understand and empathize with others' perspectives, including individuals from diverse backgrounds, cultures, and experiences. It also involves recognizing social norms, identifying available community and school resources, and demonstrating compassion and gratitude. Students with well-developed social awareness can navigate different social settings, respond appropriately to interpersonal situations, and contribute to an inclusive and supportive environment.
- *Relationship skills* refer to the ability to establish and maintain healthy, supportive relationships with peers, teachers, and the broader school community. This includes effective communication, conflict resolution, teamwork, active listening, and leadership abilities. Students with strong relationship skills can collaborate effectively, resist negative social pressures, seek help when needed, and advocate for both themselves and others in various social contexts.
- *Responsible decision-making* involves making ethical, constructive, and well-informed choices in personal and social interactions across different situations. It requires critical thinking, problem-solving, and evaluating the potential consequences of one's actions. Students with strong decision-making abilities can assess risks, analyse information, and consider the broader impact of their choices on their own well-being as well as that of others.

While initial research and intervention programmes focused on integrating SEL into student learning, more recent studies have expanded the scope of SEL beyond student development to include teachers. This shift reflects an increasing recognition that teachers' own social and emotional competencies are integral to their ability to foster SEL in students. Teachers who possess strong SEL skills are better equipped to manage classroom dynamics, engage in positive student interactions, and create emotionally supportive learning environments. Conversely, educators who lack opportunities to develop these competencies during their professional training may struggle with emotional regulation, relationship management, and classroom leadership, ultimately limiting their ability to promote SEL effectively in their students. Teachers' social and emotional skills play a crucial role in shaping not only their psychological well-being but also the broader classroom environment and students' outcomes. These competencies are essential for managing the complexities of teaching and fostering psychologically safe and emotionally supportive learning environments.

One of the earliest and most influential contributions in the field is the *Prosocial Classroom Model* proposed by Jennings and Greenberg (2009). This model represents a pivotal shift in the literature by extending the focus beyond teachers' social and emotional competencies to illustrate how these skills significantly influence a broader range of personal and professional outcomes. Specifically, the model outlines how teachers' social and emotional competencies are directly linked to their mental health, stress management, professional sustainability, and the quality of teacher-student relationships. It emphasizes the reciprocal interplay between teachers' emotional well-being and their ability to foster supportive, emotionally safe classroom environments. Table 2.2 summarizes the core competencies identified as essential for teachers to effectively regulate their own emotions and accurately perceive and respond to the emotional needs of their students.

This model highlights those teachers with high social and emotional competencies are better equipped to manage stress, prevent burnout, and sustain long-term engagement in the profession. Emotional regulation is central to this process, as it enables teachers to navigate the daily stressors of the classroom, handle disruptive behaviours, and respond to student

Table 2.2 Teacher's core competencies in managing emotions and fostering positive classroom relationships (adapted from Jennings & Greenberg, 2009)

- *Identifying and managing own emotions.* Teachers need to recognize and understand their own emotions, including their origins and consequences. They should also possess the ability to regulate emotions effectively, particularly when these emotions have the potential to be harmful to themselves or others.
- *Demonstrating enthusiasm and motivation.* Maintaining enthusiasm for teaching and learning, even in the face of frustration or setbacks, is essential. Teachers should inspire and motivate both themselves and their students to engage in the learning process, fostering resilience in challenging situations.
- *Recognizing and nurturing strengths.* Teachers should be skilled at identifying and valuing their own abilities while actively promoting the development of their student's potential. This involves encouraging students to recognize and build on their unique strengths.
- *Understanding and responding to student emotions.* The ability to perceive and appropriately respond to students' emotions is critical. Teachers should remain aware that their emotional expressions can influence students' communication and emotional responses, shaping the classroom's social-emotional climate.
- Building supportive and collaborative relationships. Developing strong, supportive relationships based on mutual understanding and collaboration is a cornerstone of effective teaching. These relationships create a foundation for trust and respect, enhancing the classroom's learning environment.
- *Conflict management and negotiation skills.* Teachers need to manage conflicts effectively by employing negotiation strategies that lead to constructive solutions. This requires maintaining a balanced and empathetic approach to resolving disagreements.
- *Appreciating diverse perspectives.* Teachers should understand and value diverse viewpoints, recognizing that differences in opinions can often stem from cultural variations. Cultivating an appreciation for diversity fosters inclusivity and a richer learning experience.
- *Modelling altruistic behaviours.* Teachers serve as role models for their students by demonstrating altruistic behaviours and promoting the development of healthy, supportive relationships. This modelling reinforces positive social norms within the classroom.
- *Making responsible decisions.* Effective teachers consider the broader implications of their decisions, ensuring that their actions positively impact both themselves and their students. This foresight underscores a commitment to ethical and empathetic teaching practices.
- *Establishing and upholding rules respectfully.* Defining and enforcing classroom rules with a respectful and fair approach is essential. Teachers must maintain a balance between authority and empathy, ensuring that students feel valued and respected within a structured environment.

needs with patience and empathy. Teachers who possess strong emotional regulation skills are less likely to experience chronic stress, emotional exhaustion, and feelings of professional dissatisfaction, all of which are significant predictors of teacher attrition. Moreover, educators with well-developed social awareness and relationship management skills are more adept at fostering supportive peer networks, seeking help when needed, and engaging in collaborative problem-solving, all of which are protective factors against occupational stress and mental health decline.

Teachers' ability to manage their own emotions directly impacts their effectiveness in classroom management. The ability to remain calm and composed during challenging interactions, engage in constructive conflict resolution, and provide consistent emotional support fosters a sense of predictability and emotional safety for students. A classroom characterized by mutual respect, trust, and emotional stability is less likely to experience high levels of student misbehaviour, disengagement, and emotional distress. Conversely, teachers who struggle with stress management and emotional self-regulation may inadvertently contribute to a tense and unpredictable classroom climate, which can exacerbate student anxiety, defiance, and learning difficulties. The Prosocial Classroom Model also underscores the importance of teacher social and emotional skills in sustaining professional commitment and preventing burnout as teachers who lack adequate skills to regulate emotions, seek social support, and develop adaptive coping mechanisms are at a greater risk of experiencing burnout, job dissatisfaction, and premature exit from the profession.

Recent meta-analyses and systematic reviews have substantially deepened our understanding of the impact of SEL interventions on teachers' personal and professional functioning. These studies consistently highlight that programmes aimed at enhancing social and emotional competencies yield measurable and meaningful benefits across various psychological and occupational domains. In particular, a comprehensive meta-analysis by Oliveira et al. (2021a), which examined 43 studies involving more than 3000 in-service teachers, found that SEL interventions led to statistically significant improvements in teachers' social and emotional competence and reductions in psychological distress. These outcomes were reflected in small-to-moderate effect sizes, a statistical indicator of the magnitude of an intervention's impact. Such effect sizes suggest that, on average, teachers who participated in SEL programmes experienced meaningful improvements compared to those in control groups.

At the personal level, several meta-analytic findings converge in demonstrating that SEL interventions contribute to a decrease in psychological distress. These improvements encompass reductions in negative affect including, for instance, aversive emotional states such as sadness, anxiety, anger, and guilt, as well as decreases in stress, depressive symptoms, and emotional exhaustion (Iancu et al., 2018; Oliveira et al., 2021b; Roeser et al., 2013). SEL interventions have also shown a positive effect on personal accomplishment, which refers to teachers' perceived sense of competence, professional efficacy, and fulfilment in their role. Higher levels of personal accomplishment are strongly associated with enhanced job satisfaction, intrinsic motivation, and resilience in the face of occupational challenges. Both Oliveira et al. (2021a) and Iancu et al. (2018) found that SEL programmes led to improvements in this area, suggesting that such interventions can play a critical role in reinforcing teachers' sense of professional purpose and engagement.

Beyond psychological benefits, SEL interventions have also demonstrated promising effects on physiological indicators of stress and physical health. Teachers who completed SEL programmes reported fewer somatic complaints, such as headaches and insomnia, and exhibited improved physiological regulation, including more balanced cortisol levels and heart rate variability (Harris et al., 2016). These findings support the conceptualization of social and emotional competencies as a protective factor that can mitigate the cumulative physiological toll of sustained occupational stress. Moreover, SEL interventions have been linked to enhancements in general well-being. Participants commonly report increased positive affect, stronger self-efficacy beliefs, greater job satisfaction, and improved life satisfaction (Oliveira et al., 2021a). These outcomes are especially important in sustaining long-term professional engagement. Particularly, teachers with higher self-efficacy are more likely to feel fulfilled in their role and remain committed to their profession over time (Crain et al., 2017).

Finally, the positive effects of SEL interventions are influenced by several implementation-related factors. Among these, intervention duration has emerged as a key moderator. According to Iancu et al. (2018), interventions lasting longer than 1 month produced greater reductions in emotional exhaustion and more substantial increases in personal accomplishment compared to shorter programmes. Additionally, the alignment of content with teachers' specific educational levels and the inclusion of structured follow-up sessions further enhance intervention efficacy. These findings suggest that both duration and the quality of SEL implementation are critical to maximizing its impact on teacher outcomes.

References

American Psychiatric Association. (2022). *Diagnostic and statistical manual of mental disorders* (5th ed. (text revision) ed.). APA Publishing.

Andres, P., Dobrovská, D., & Vaněček, D. (2023). Victims of educator-targeted bullying: A qualitative study on teacher harmful experience. In M. Auer, P. Wolfgang, & T. Rüütmann (Eds.), *Learning in the age of digital and green transition* (pp. 729–734). Springer.

Anonymous. (1906). Mental health of school children. *Journal of the American Medical Association, XLVII*(1), 39–40. https://doi.org/10.1001/jama.1906.02520010047005

Arnow, B., Kenardy, J., & Agras, W. S. (1995). The emotional eating scale: The development of a measure to assess coping with negative affect by eating. *International Journal of Eating Disorders, 18*(1), 79–90. https://doi.org/10.3280/10.1002/1098-108x(199507)18:1<79::aid-eat2260180109>3.0.co;2-v

Avanzi, L., Balducci, C., & Fraccaroli, F. (2013). *Contributo alla validazione italiana del Copenhagen Burnout Inventory (CBI)* [Contribution to the Italian validation of the Copenhagen Burnout Inventory (CBI)]. *Psicologia della Salute, 2013*, 120–135. https://doi.org/10.3280/PDS2013-002008

Bakker, A. B., & Demerouti, E. (2007). The job demands-resources model: State of the art. *Journal of Managerial Psychology, 22*(3), 309–328. https://doi.org/10.1108/02683940710733115

Beltman, S. (2015). Teacher professional resilience: Thriving not just surviving. In N. Weatherby-Fell (Ed.), *Learning to teach in the secondary school* (pp. 20–38). Cambridge University Press.

Beltman, S., Mansfield, C., & Price, A. (2011). Thriving not just surviving: A review of research on teacher resilience. *Educational Research Review, 6*(3), 185–207. https://doi.org/10.1016/j.edurev.2011.09.001

Blase, J., & Blase, J. (2002). The dark side of leadership: Teacher perspectives of principal mistreatment. *Educational Administration Quarterly, 38*(5), 671–727. https://doi.org/10.1177/0013161X02239643

Blase, J., & Blase, J. (2006). Teachers-perspectives on principal mistreatment. *Teacher Education Quarterly, 33*(4), 123–142.

Block, J., & Kremen, A. M. (1996). IQ and ego-resiliency: Conceptual and empirical connections and separateness. *Journal of Personality and Social Psychology, 70*(2), 349–361. https://doi.org/10.1037/0022-3514.70.2.349

Burns, E., Fogelgarn, R., & Billett, P. (2020). Teacher-targeted bullying and harassment in Australian schools: A challenge to teacher wellbeing. *British Journal of Sociology of Education, 41*(4), 523–538. https://doi.org/10.1080/01425692.2020.1755227

Burns, E., Fogelgarn, R., & Billett, P. (2024). Men school teachers get bullied too: Examples from an Australian study. *International Journal of Qualitative Studies in Education, 38*(2), 267–281. https://doi.org/10.1080/09518398.2024.2365922

Cavioni, V., & Grazzani, I. (2023). *L'apprendimento sociale ed emotivo: Teorie e buone pratiche per promuovere la salute mentale a scuola [Social and emotional learning: Theories and best practices for promoting mental health at school].* Il Mulino.

Cavioni, V., Grazzani, I., & Ornaghi, V. (2020). Mental health promotion in schools: A comprehensive theoretical framework. *International Journal of Emotional Education, 12*(1), 65–82.

Cavioni, V., Grazzani, I., Ornaghi, V., Agliati, A., Gandellini, S., Cefai, C., et al. (2023a). A multi-component curriculum to promote teachers' mental health: Findings from the PROMEHS program. *The International Journal of Emotional Education, 15*(1), 34–52. https://doi.org/10.56300/KFNZ2526

Cavioni, V., Toto, G., & Ornaghi, V. (2023b). Portraits of pre-service special education teachers: Clustered perspectives on their well-being and its association with self-efficacy and commitment to work. *International Journal of Emotional Education, 15*(2), 21–36. https://doi.org/10.56300/VHRV8364

Cavioni, V., Ornaghi, V., & Conte, E. (2024). Promoting teachers' well-being through a serious game intervention: A qualitative exploration of teachers' experiences. *Frontiers in Psychology, 15*, 1339242. https://doi.org/10.3389/fpsyg.2024.1339242

Cefai, C., & Cavioni, V. (2014). *Social and emotional education in primary school. Integrating theory and research into practice*. Springer.

Cefai, C., Cavioni, V., Bartolo, P., & Simoes, C. (2021). RESCUR surfing the waves: A resilience program for social inclusion and social justice. In P. Liamputtong (Ed.), *Handbook of social inclusion, research and practices in health and social care* (pp. 1–14). Springer Nature. https://doi.org/10.1007/978-3-030-48277-0_111-1

Chang, M.-L. (2009). An appraisal perspective of teacher burnout: Examining the emotional work of teachers. *Educational Psychology Review, 21*(3), 193–218. https://doi.org/10.1007/s10648-009-9106-y

Cho, C. L., & Corkett, J. K. (2023). *Global perspectives on microaggressions in higher education understanding and combating covert violence in universities*. Routledge.

Coetzee, M., & van Dyk, J. (2018). Workplace bullying and turnover intention: Exploring work engagement as a potential mediator. *Psychological Reports, 121*(2), 375–392. https://doi.org/10.1177/0033294117725073

Crain, T. L., Schonert-Reichl, K. A., & Roeser, R. W. (2017). Cultivating teacher mindfulness: Effects of a randomized controlled trial on work, home, and sleep outcomes. *Journal of Occupational Health Psychology, 22*(2), 138–152. https://doi.org/10.1037/ocp0000043

De Wet, C. (2010). Victims of educator-targeted bullying: A qualitative study. *South African Journal of Education, 30*, 189–201.

Denham, S. A., Bassett, H. H., Zinsser, K., & Wyatt, T. M. (2014). How preschoolers' social-emotional learning predicts their early school success: Developing theory-promoting, competency-based assessments. *Infant and Child Development, 23*(4), 426–454. https://doi.org/10.1002/icd.1840

Downes, P., & Cefai, C. (2016). *How to prevent and tackle bullying and school violence: Evidence and practices for strategies for inclusive and safe schools, NESET II Report*. Publications Office of the European Union. https://doi.org/10.2766/079

Durlak, J. A., Domitrovich, C. E., & Mahoney, J. L. (2024). *Handbook of social and emotional learning* (2nd ed.). Guildford Press.

Escobar Lux, M., Mayorga Merino, M., Viviescas, A., & Escobar, J. M. (2023). The other pandemic: Mental illness in young people from low and middle-income countries. *Current Opinion in Psychology, 52*, 101642. https://doi.org/10.1016/j.copsyc.2023.101642

Fan, C., Fu, P., Li, X., Li, M., & Zhu, M. (2021). Trauma exposure and the PTSD symptoms of college teachers during the peak of the COVID-19 outbreak. *Stress Health, 37*(5), 914–927. https://doi.org/10.1002/smi.3049

Folkman, S., & Lazarus, R. S. (1988). Coping as a mediator of emotion. *Journal of Personality and Social Psychology, 54*(3), 466–475. https://pubmed.ncbi.nlm.nih.gov/3361419

Gallant, A., & Riley, P. (2014). Early career teacher attrition: New thoughts on an intractable problem. *Teacher Development, 18*(4), 562.580. https://doi.org/10.1080/13664530.2014.945129

Gavin, B., Lyne, J., & McNicholas, F. (2020). Mental health and the COVID-19 pandemic. *Irish Journal of Psychological Medicine, 37*(3), 156–158. https://doi.org/10.1017/ipm.2020.72

Gavin, B., Lyne, J., & McNicholas, F. (2021). The global impact on mental health almost 2 years into the COVID-19 pandemic. *Irish Journal of Psychological Medicine, 38*(4), 243–246. https://doi.org/10.1017/ipm.2021.75

Giorgi, I., Mainetti, P., Fiabane, E., Bertolotti, E., Baiardi, P., Massidda, D., et al. (2014). Discriminant capacity of the masi-r questionnaire for the perceived work stress assessment. *Giornale Italiano di Medicina del Lavoro ed Ergonomia, 36*(3), 175–180.

Gross, J. J., & John, O. P. (2003). Individual differences in two emotion regulation processes: Implications for affect, relationships, and well-being. *Journal of Personality and Social Psychology, 85*(2), 348–362. https://doi.org/10.1037/0022-3514.85.2.348

Gu, Q., & Day, C. (2007). Teachers resilience: A necessary condition for effectiveness. *Teaching and Teacher Education, 23*, 1302–1316. https://doi.org/10.1016/j.tate.2006.06.00

Hakanen, J. J., Bakker, A. B., & Schaufeli, W. B. (2006). Burnout and work engagement among teachers. *Journal of School Psychology, 43*(6), 495–513. https://doi.org/10.1016/j.jsp.2005.11.001

Harris, A. R., Jennings, P. A., Katz, D. A., Abenavoli, R. M., & Greenberg, M. T. (2016). Promoting stress management and wellbeing in educators: Feasibility and efficacy of a school-based yoga and mindfulness intervention. *Mindfulness, 7*(1), 143–154. https://doi.org/10.1007/s12671-015-0451-2

Höltge, J., Jefferies, P., Cowden, R. G., Govender, K., Maximo, S. I., Carranza, J. S., et al. (2021). A cross-country network analysis of adolescent resilience. *Journal of Adolescent Health, 68*(3), 580–588. https://doi.org/10.1016/j.jadohealth.2020.07.010

Iancu, A. E., Rusu, A., Măroiu, C., PăPăcurar, R., & Maricuțoiu, L. P. (2018). The effectiveness of interventions aimed at reducing teacher burnout: A meta-analysis. *Educational Psychology Review, 30*(2), 373–396. https://doi.org/10.1007/s10648-017-9420-8

Idoiaga Mondragon, N., Fernandez, I. L., Ozamiz-Etxebarria, N., Villagrasa, B., & Santabárbara, J. (2023). PTSD (Posttraumatic Stress Disorder) in teachers: A mini meta-analysis during COVID-19. *International Journal of Environmental Research and Public Health, 20*(3), 1802. https://doi.org/10.3390/ijerph20031802

Jennings, P. A. (2020). *Teacher burnout turnaround. Strategies for empowered educators.* Norton Books.

Jennings, P. A., & Greenberg, M. T. (2009). The Prosocial Classroom: Teacher social and emotional competence in relation to student and classroom outcomes. *Review of Educational Research, 79*(1), 491–525. https://doi.org/10.3102/0034654308325693

Kauppi, T., & Pörhölä, M. (2012). Teachers bullied by students: Forms of bullying and perpetrator characteristics. *Violence and Victims, 27*(3), 396–413. https://doi.org/10.1891/0886-6708.27.3.396

Keashly, L. (1998). Emotional abuse in the workplace: Conceptual and empirical issues. *Journal of Emotional Abuse, 1*(1), 85–117. https://doi.org/10.1300/J135v01n01_05

Keyes, C. L. M. (2002). The mental health continuum: From languishing to flourishing in life. *Journal of Health and Behavior Research, 43*, 207–222.

Lazarus, R., & Folkman, S. (1984). *Stress: Appraisal and coping.* Springer.

Luthar, S. S., & Zelazo, L. B. (2003). Research on resilience: An integrative review. In S. S. Luthar (Ed.), *Resilience and vulnerability: Adaptation in the context of childhood adversities* (pp. 510–549). Cambridge University Press. https://doi.org/10.1017/CBO9780511615788.023

Mahoney, J. L., Weissberg, R. P., Greenberg, M. T., Dusenbury, L., Jagers, R. J., Niemi, K., Schlinger, M., Schlund, J., Shriver, T. P., VanAusdal, K., & Yoder, N. (2021). Systemic social and emotional learning: Promoting educational success for all preschool to high school students. *American Psychologist, 76*(7), 1128–1142. https://doi.org/10.1037/amp0000701

Mansfield, C. F., Beltman, S., Price, A., & McConney, A. (2012). "Don't sweat the small stuff": Understanding teacher resilience at the chalkface. *Teaching and Teacher Education, 28*(3), 357–367. https://doi.org/10.1016/j.tate.2011.11.001

Mansfield, C. F., Beltman, S., Broadley, T., & Weatherby-Fell, N. (2016). Building resilience in teacher education: An evidenced informed framework. *Teaching and Teacher Education, 54*, 77–87. https://doi.org/10.1016/j.tate.2015.11.016

Maslach, C. (1982). *Burn-out: The cost of caring.* Prentice Hall.

Maslach, C., Schaufeli, W. B., & Leiter, M. P. (2001). Job burnout. *Annual Review of Psychology, 52*, 397–422. https://doi.org/10.1146/annurev.psych.52.1.397

Masten, A. S. (2001). Ordinary magic. Resilience processes in development. *American Psychologist, 56*(3), 227–238. https://doi.org/10.1037/0003-066X.56.3.227

Matsui, J. (2005). *Bullying in the workplace. A survey of Ontario's elementary and secondary school teachers and education workers.* English Catholic Teachers' Association (OECTA).

McEwen, B. S. (1998). Stress, adaptation, and disease. Allostasis and allostatic load. *Annals New York Acad Sciences, 1*(840), 33–44. https://doi.org/10.1111/j.1749-6632.1998.tb09546.x

Michie, S., & Cockcroft, A. (1996). Overwork can kill. *British Medical Journal, 312*(7036), 921–922. https://doi.org/10.1136/bmj.312.7036.921

Miller, D. S. (2024). The retention and attrition of early-career music teachers: A survival analysis. *Arts Education Policy Review, 126*(1), 1–17. https://doi.org/10.1080/10632913.2024.2329699

Murphy, C. (2024). *Cyberbullying among young people: Laws and policies in selected member states.* EPRS European Parliamentary Research Service. Retrieved February 17, 2025, https://www.europarl.europa.eu/RegData/etudes/BRIE/2024/762331/EPRS_BRI(2024)762331_EN.pdf

Oliveira, S., Roberto, M. S., Pereira, N. S., Marques-Pinto, A., & Veiga-Simão, A. M. (2021a). Impacts of social and emotional learning interventions for teachers on teachers' outcomes: A systematic review with meta-analysis. *Frontiers in Psychology, 12*, 677217. https://doi.org/10.3389/fpsyg.2021.677217

Oliveira, S., Roberto, M. S., Veiga-Simão, A. M., & Marques-Pinto, A. (2021b). A meta-analysis of the impact of social and emotional learning interventions on teachers' burnout symptoms. *Educational Psychology Review, 33*, 1779–1808. https://doi.org/10.1007/s10648-021-09612-x

Olweus, D. (1994). *Bullying at school.* Blackwell Publishers.

Orange, A. (2018). Workplace bullying in schools: Teachers' perceptions of why they were mistreated. *The Educational Forum, 82*(4), 390–405. https://doi.org/10.1080/00131725.2018.1461523

Ornaghi, V., Conte, E., Agliati, A., & Gandellini, S. (2022). Early-childhood teachers' emotion socialization practices: A multi-method study. *Early Child Development and Care, 192*(10), 1608–1625. https://doi.org/10.1080/03004430.2021.1918124

Ornaghi, V., Conte, E., Cavioni, V., Farina, E., & Pepe, A. (2023). The role of teachers' socio-emotional competence in reducing burnout through increased work engagement. *Frontiers in Psychology, 14*, 1295365. https://doi.org/10.3389/fpsyg.2023.1295365

Özgenel, M., & Aksu, T. (2020). The power of school principals' ethical leadership behavior to predict organizational health. *International Journal of Evaluation and Research in Education, 9*(4), 816–825. https://doi.org/10.11591/ijere.v9i4.20658

Pearson, C. M., Andersson, L. M., & Wegner, M. J. (2001). When workers flout convention: A study of workplace incivility. *Human Relations, 54*, 1387–1419. https://doi.org/10.1177/00187267015411001

Petrillo, G., Capone, V., Caso, D., & Keyes, C. L. M. (2015). The Mental Health Continuum–Short Form (MHC–SF) as a measure of well-being in the Italian context. *Social Indicators Research, 121*(1), 291–312. https://doi.org/10.1007/s11205-014-0629-3

Roeser, R. W., Schonert-Reichl, K. A., Jha, A., Cullen, M., Wallace, L., Wilensky, R., et al. (2013). Mindfulness training and reductions in teacher stress and burnout: Results from two randomized, waitlist-control field trials. *Journal of Educational Psychology, 105*(3), 787–804. https://doi.org/10.1037/a0032093

Salmi, V., & Kivivuori, J. (2009). *Opettajiin kohdistuva häirintä ja väkivalta 2008 [Harassment and violence directed at teachers 2008]*. National Research Institute of Legal Policy. Retrieved February 17, 2025, from https://helda.helsinki.fi/server/api/core/bitstreams/1a41442e-fed9-4929-8cc5-b3903688780c/content

Schaefer, L. (2013). Beginning teacher attrition: A question of identity making and identity shifting. *Teachers and Teaching, 19*(3), 260–274. https://doi.org/10.1080/13540602.2012.754159

Schonert-Reichl, K. A., Kitil, M. J., & Hanson-Peterson, J. (2017). *To reach the students, teach the teachers: A national scan of teacher preparation and social and emotional learning. A report prepared for the Collaborative for Academic, Social, and Emotional Learning (CASEL)*. University of British Columbia.

Schwarzer, R., & Hallum, S. (2008). Perceived teacher self-efficacy as a predictor of job stress and burnout. *Applied Psychology: An International Review, 57*(Suppl. 1), 152–171. https://doi.org/10.1111/j.1464-0597.2008.00359.x

Stamate, A.-N., Brunet, L., & Savoie, A. (2015). La compétence en emploi peut-elle prédire la santépsychologique des enseignants? [Can job competence predict the psychological health of teachers?]. *Le travail humain, 4*(78), 355–378. https://doi.org/10.3917/th.784.0355

Sun, M. D., & Rieder, E. A. (2021). Stress, skin, and beauty: The basic science base. In E. A. Rieder & R. G. Fried (Eds.), *Essential psychiatry for the aesthetic practitioner* (pp. 3–21). Wiley Blackwell. https://doi.org/10.1002/9781119680116.ch1

Tait, M. (2008). Resilience as a contributor to novice teacher success, commitment, and retention. *Teacher Education Quarterly, 35*(4), 57–75.

Terry, A. A. (1998). Teachers as targets of bullying by their pupils: A study to investigate incidence. *British Journal of Educational Psychology, 68*(2), 255–268. https://doi.org/10.1111/j.2044-8279.1998.tb01288.x

UNESCO. (2024). *Safe to learn and thrive ending violence in and through education.* United Nations Educational, Scientific and Cultural Organization. https://doi.org/10.54675/LUPY3293

Ungar, M. (2018). Systemic resilience: Principles and processes for a science of change in contexts of adversity. *Ecology and Society, 23*(4). https://doi.org/10.5751/ES-10385-230434

Weare, K. (2010). Mental health and social and emotional learning: Evidence, principles, tensions, balances. *Advances in School Mental Health Promotion, 3*(1), 5–17. https://doi.org/10.1080/1754730X.2010.9715670

Westphal, A., Kalinowski, E., Hoferichter, C. J., & Vock, M. (2022). K-12 teachers' stress and burnout during the COVID-19 pandemic: A systematic review. *Frontiers in Psychology, 13*, 920326. https://doi.org/10.3389/fpsyg.2022.920326

World Health Organization (WHO). (2005). *Promoting mental health: Concepts, emerging evidence, practice.* World Health Organization.

Yildirim, K. (2014). Main factors of teachers' professional well-being. *Educational Research and Reviews, 9*(6), 153–163.

Zanetti, M. A., & Caravita, S. C. S. (2018). Il cyberbullismo come emergenza sociale: Indicazioni per l'intervento alla luce della nuova normative [Cyberbullying as a social emergency: Indications for intervention in light of the new legislation]. *Maltrattamento e Abuso all'Infanzia, 20*(1), 7. https://doi.org/10.3280/MAL2018-001001

Zheng, M., Asif, M., Tufail, M. S., Naseer, S., Khokhar, S. G., Chen, X., & Naveed, R. T. (2022). COVID Academic pandemic: Techno stress faced by teaching staff for online academic activities. *Frontiers in Psychology, 13*, 895371. https://doi.org/10.3389/fpsyg.2022.895371

Zurlo, M. C., Pes, D., & Capasso, R. (2016). Personality characteristics, job stressors, and job satisfaction: Main and interaction effects on psychological and physical health conditions of Italian schoolteachers. *Psychological Reports, 119*(1), 27–38. https://doi.org/10.1177/0033294116656818

3

Nurturing Relationships in the Classroom: Dynamics of Emotional Connections

Abstract This chapter explores how emotionally supportive teachers not only enhance student well-being but also experience positive effects on their own psychological health. Additionally, the chapter focuses on the concept of the "teacher's invisible hand", emphasizing the subtle ways in which educators shape classroom dynamics and influence academic success. Furthermore, a qualitative study is presented, analysing teachers' positive and negative recollections of their own school experiences to investigate their impact on educational trajectories, as well as personal and professional identity formation.

Keywords Teacher-student relationships • Self-regulation • Emotional support • Sense of community • Academic achievement • School memories

V. Cavioni, *Fostering Teachers' Mental Health*,
https://doi.org/10.1007/978-3-031-92571-9_3

3.1 Beyond Instruction: The Reciprocal Impact of Teacher-Student Relationships

A substantial body of empirical research underscores the critical role of high-quality teacher-student relationships in shaping students' cognitive, social, emotional, and academic development (Pianta et al., 2003). Emotionally competent teachers play a fundamental role in fostering student well-being, and, in turn, these relationships also contribute significantly to teachers' psychological health and professional fulfilment (Antognazza, 2017). The reciprocal nature of teacher-student interactions is increasingly recognized, highlighting their long-term implications not only for students but also for teachers themselves. Warm, structured, and supportive teacher-student interactions act as a protective factor for students, particularly those from socioeconomically disadvantaged backgrounds or those with adverse childhood experiences (Sabol et al., 2013). A nurturing and emotionally responsive dynamic is associated with improved academic performance and reductions in both externalizing behaviours (e.g., conduct problems, aggression) and internalizing symptoms (e.g., anxiety, depression) (Maldonado-Carreño & Votruba-Drzal, 2011). Furthermore, students exhibiting social withdrawal or depressive symptoms benefit significantly from secure and trusting relationships with their teachers, which lower the risk of developing long-term psychopathology (O'Connor et al., 2011).

Beyond individual student outcomes, teacher-student relationships shape the broader classroom climate. The "teacher's invisible hand" (Farmer et al., 2011; Endedijk et al., 2022) describes how teachers subtly influence peer interactions, either fostering inclusion and social cohesion or inadvertently reinforcing exclusionary dynamics. Positive teacher-student relationships promote peer acceptance and social integration, while conflictual interactions have been linked to peer rejection and increased externalizing behaviours, such as aggression and classroom disruption.

However, the impact of teacher-student relationships extends beyond students, directly influencing teachers' resilience, job satisfaction, and long-term engagement in the profession. While much of the literature has focused on student outcomes, growing evidence highlights the bidirectional nature of these interactions and their effect on teachers' psychological well-being. Educators who establish emotionally supportive relationships with their students experience lower levels of stress, burnout, and job dissatisfaction (Arens & Morin, 2016). Conversely, conflictual teacher-student interactions, particularly in classrooms with high behavioural challenges, have been associated with heightened emotional exhaustion, reduced professional fulfilment, and increased attrition rates (Grayson & Alvarez, 2008). Teachers frequently exposed to student defiance, resistance, or aggression face greater psychological distress, reinforcing the urgent need for relational competence and emotional regulation skills as protective factors against burnout. At the same time, positive relationships with students can be a source of resilience and motivation, particularly in challenging educational settings. Many educators find inspiration and renewed purpose in witnessing students overcome adversity, reinforcing their commitment to teaching. Teachers who foster strong connections with students and their families report higher levels of professional fulfilment, as these relationships serve as a buffer against occupational stress, helping them maintain engagement despite systemic and contextual challenges.

The teacher-student relationship is not merely a determinant of student success but a dynamic and reciprocal interaction that also influences teachers' well-being, motivation, and career sustainability. Understanding this interdependence is crucial, as the following sections will explore how the quality of this relationship impacts key aspects of student development while also shaping teachers' psychological well-being and professional fulfilment.

3.1.1 The Role of Teacher-Student Interactions in Supporting Self-Regulation Development

The research underscores the significant role of high-quality teacher-student interactions in fostering students' self-regulation, particularly in early childhood education. Self-regulation refers to the capacity to control one's thoughts, emotions, and actions. It includes key skills such as attentional control, impulse inhibition, cognitive flexibility, and goal-directed behaviour, enabling individuals to achieve personal objectives and adapt effectively to different situations (Baumeister & Vohs, 2004). This skill develops through interactions influenced by various factors, including knowledge and experience acquired within the family (genetic predispositions and caregiving), interactions with teachers, peers, and playmates, as well as engagement with the physical environment and materials such as books and toys.

The quality of teacher-child relationships plays a particularly protective role for children who begin preschool with lower self-regulation skills. Cadima et al. (2016) found that instructional support, which is the extent to which teachers engage children in meaningful learning experiences through structured guidance, thought-provoking discussions, and cognitively stimulating activities, had a greater impact on children with initially weak self-regulation abilities. This suggests that well-structured and supportive classroom environments can act as compensatory contexts, helping to bridge developmental gaps and promote cognitive and emotional growth. At the same time, children's ability to regulate attention and control impulses is a key factor in shaping the quality of their social interactions (Williford et al., 2013). Those who can effectively focus and manage their impulses tend to engage more positively with their teachers, fostering richer learning experiences. Ocak (2010) further demonstrated that children who actively participate in positive teacher interactions exhibit stronger problem-solving skills, a core component of executive functions, and show greater cognitive flexibility by generating a higher number of ideas. Similarly, Hamre et al. (2013) examined a large sample of preschool children and found that those in classrooms with more sensitive and responsive teachers demonstrated stronger executive function abilities, reinforcing the importance of teacher-child interactions in early development.

Children from socially *disadvantaged backgrounds* particularly benefit from emotionally supportive teacher interactions, which act as a protective factor in the development of self-regulation. Research highlights that teacher support is especially beneficial for children exposed to multiple risk factors, such as socioeconomic hardship and inconsistent caregiving environments (Cadima et al., 2016). Specifically, children who experience warm, responsive, and nurturing interactions with their teachers develop stronger attentional control, working memory, and inhibitory control. Working memory refers to the ability to temporarily hold and manipulate information while performing cognitive tasks, such as following multi-step instructions, solving problems, or engaging in reasoning. These executive functions are essential for self-regulation, learning, and adaptive behaviours. In this context, positive teacher-student relationships act as external scaffolding, providing temporary, structured support that helps children gradually develop independent self-regulation skills. In classrooms where teachers actively encourage reasoning, provide clear and structured feedback, and engage children in cognitively stimulating interactions, young learners have more opportunities to develop executive function skills. These structured and responsive learning environments counteract the negative effects of early adversity by promoting children's ability to sustain attention, regulate impulses, and engage in goal-directed behaviour. Thus, through guided emotional and behavioural support, teachers help children internalize strategies for managing their emotions, and behaviours and fostering greater autonomy.

The advantages of positive teacher-student interactions extend beyond preschool and into the early years of formal education. In kindergarten, instructional support has been directly associated with enhancements in executive functioning, a set of cognitive processes fundamental to self-regulation. These processes, including working memory, cognitive flexibility, and inhibitory control, continue to develop throughout primary school and are crucial for adaptive learning and behavioural regulation (Silinskas et al., 2017).

3.1.2 The Impact of Emotionally Supportive, Structured, and Responsive Teaching

High-quality interactions characterized by *emotional warmth, structure, and responsiveness* provide a foundation for social and emotional development, while also supporting students' ability to cope with academic challenges and regulate their behaviour effectively (Hofkens et al., 2023). Emotional warmth encompasses teachers' ability to express genuine care, empathy, and positive regard towards students and fosters psychological safety as well as reducing anxiety and promoting prosocial behaviours. Emotional support has been also found to mitigate the risk of disengagement and avoidance behaviours in response to academic challenges. For example, students who experience low levels of emotional support in early elementary school are more likely to exhibit task avoidance and passive disengagement in later academic settings (Pakarinen et al., 2014). Emotional support in the classroom fosters a sense of trust and security, strengthening students' perceptions of their teachers as caring and fair. This aspect is particularly crucial for students at risk of disengagement, as a supportive classroom climate helps buffer against the development of negative attitudes towards teachers. Students who perceive their teachers as emotionally supportive are less likely to view their actions as unjust or overly punitive, which helps prevent disengagement and fosters long-term academic motivation (Gasser et al., 2018). Furthermore, when teachers are seen as fair and compassionate, students are more inclined to follow classroom expectations, show respect towards peers and educators, and adopt social norms that contribute to a positive and inclusive school environment (Hughes et al., 2008).

Emotionally supportive teacher-student interactions play a crucial role in adolescence, as they are strongly linked to increased engagement, higher academic motivation, and a stronger sense of belonging within the school environment (Pöysä et al., 2019). Given that adolescence is a developmental stage marked by the search for autonomy and identity formation, there is a common assumption that teachers should adopt an emotionally distant approach to encourage students' independence. This perspective often leads to the misconception that fostering autonomy necessitates a lack of affective connection or emotional detachment. However, research indicates that rather than emotional distance, adolescents benefit most from emotionally available teachers, providing both guidance and support while respecting their growing need for independence (Cavioni et al., 2021). Despite the importance of these relationships, studies suggest that their quality tends to decline during adolescence, with students perceiving them as less fulfilling over time. This trend is particularly evident among male students, who often report lower levels of emotional support and attunement from their teachers. Consequently, the emotional closeness of a supportive teacher does not hinder autonomy; rather, it creates a psychologically safe environment where students feel empowered to take risks, engage in self-reflection, and navigate the complexities of personal and academic challenges. In this sense, the teacher's role is not to replace adolescent independence but to act as a stabilizing force, providing reassurance and scaffolding as students progressively develop confidence in their own abilities. Thus, rather than viewing emotional warmth as incompatible with adolescent autonomy, it should be recognized as an essential component of students' social and emotional development.

Structured classroom environments play a crucial role in shaping students' social behaviour by establishing clear expectations, consistent routines, and well-defined behavioural guidelines. These elements foster self-discipline, impulse control, and goal-directed behaviour, providing a stable foundation for emotional, social and academic development. For young children, such structured settings enhance their adaptability, ease transitions, reinforce social norms, and promote cooperative learning (Bodrova & Leong, 2006). Additionally, structured classroom environments are associated with higher learning motivation in kindergarteners and contribute to greater cognitive and behavioural engagement among secondary school students (Pöysä et al., 2019).

Responsive teaching, defined as a teacher's ability to attune to students' individual needs and adapt instructional strategies, accordingly, plays a critical role in fostering academic motivation, social development, and overall student outcomes (Wentzel, 2015). By providing structured, cognitively stimulating, and emotionally supportive instruction, teachers create an environment that promotes student engagement, facilitates cooperative learning, and strengthens emotional regulation in social interactions. When students perceive their teachers as responsive, they are more likely to experience a sense of competence, autonomy, and relatedness, which enhances their intrinsic motivation, persistence in challenging tasks, and overall engagement in the learning process. From the teacher's perspective, engaging in responsive teaching not only benefits students but also has significant implications for educators' psychological well-being. Teachers who establish meaningful and attuned interactions with their students often experience a greater sense of professional efficacy, job satisfaction, and emotional fulfilment. Teachers may feel a stronger sense of purpose and accomplishment, which acts as a protective factor against emotional exhaustion and burnout (Spilt et al., 2011).

Moreover, responsiveness in teaching enhances teachers' capacity for emotional self-regulation, allowing them to navigate classroom challenges with greater resilience and adaptability.

Figure 3.1, a drawing created by an in-service teacher during a professional development course, visually exemplifies the concept of responsive teaching. The task required participants to create a figurative representation of how they perceive themselves as teachers of their students. In this particular illustration, the teacher depicted themselves as an anchor, symbolizing stability, support, and grounding for students in their learning journey (Cavioni & Toto, 2024). This metaphor aligns closely with the principles of responsive teaching, which emphasizes the importance of

Fig. 3.1 The teacher as an anchor: A metaphor for responsive teaching (Cavioni & Toto, 2024, p. 98)

providing a structured yet flexible environment where students feel secure, understood, and guided. The anchor serves as a stabilizing force, ensuring that students do not feel adrift in the challenges of academic and social development. A teacher who sees themselves as an anchor likely perceives their role as one of emotional availability, academic scaffolding, and consistent support. Moreover, this representation highlights how responsive teaching fosters both autonomy and security. Just as an anchor does not prevent a ship from moving but rather provides a steady point of reference, a responsive teacher does not impose rigid control over students but instead offers the emotional and instructional grounding necessary for them to explore, take risks, and build confidence in their abilities.

The teacher's self-perception as an anchor also suggests a strong sense of professional identity and commitment to student-centred teaching. Thus, the anchor metaphor not only represents the teacher's function in students' development but also reflects the reciprocal benefits of responsive teaching for educators themselves.

3.1.3 Building a Supportive School Community

In the school context, the sense of community is defined as students' perception of being valued, accepted, and emotionally connected within their learning environment (Cavioni & Grazzani, 2023). Sense of community is composed of four interrelated dimensions that collectively model students' experiences in school. The first dimension, *belonging*, refers to the extent to which students feel part of and identify with their school community. This sense of affiliation makes students more likely to participate actively in school activities, engage with peers, and trust their educators. The second dimension, *emotional connection*, pertains to the meaningful affective bonds that students develop within the school environment. This includes not only peer friendships but also positive interactions with teachers and the other members of school staff who can provide support and guidance. Third, *physical safety* plays a crucial role in fostering sense of community, as students must perceive their school as a secure and protective space where they feel free from bullying, discrimination, or threats to their well-being. A safe school climate ensures that students can focus on learning rather than being preoccupied with self-protection. Lastly, the dimension of *opportunity* refers to students' belief in their ability to influence their surroundings and meet both personal and collective needs. A strong sense of agency within the school environment reinforces students' motivation to take initiative, voice their opinions, and actively contribute to classroom and school-wide discussions.

Students who develop a strong sense of community are more likely to demonstrate academic motivation, maintain consistent school attendance, and establish positive peer relationships. A heightened sense of community is also associated with increased prosocial behaviours, including supporting peers in distress, demonstrating respect towards classmates and teachers, and embracing diversity within the school community (Murray & Greenberg, 2000). Additionally, a well-established sense of community acts as a psychological buffer against academic stress and school-related anxiety, reducing students' vulnerability to disengagement and emotional distress. When students perceive their school as a welcoming and inclusive space, they are less likely to experience social isolation and more likely to develop resilience in the face of educational challenges. Furthermore, students with a strong sense of community exhibit lower tendencies towards risky behaviours, such as substance use, delinquency, or school dropout, reinforcing the protective function of a supportive educational environment.

Figure 3.2 presents a photograph from Mismatched Socks Day, an annual event promoting diversity and inclusion. This initiative encourages students to embrace individuality, symbolizing that true harmony lies in celebrating differences. What may seem like a playful activity gains deeper significance within the sense of community framework. Wearing mismatched socks fosters belonging, reinforcing that every student is a valued member of the school, regardless of background or abilities. The activity strengthens emotional connections, creating a warm and accepting atmosphere in which students bond with peers and teachers. Seeing classmates and educators participate enhances unity and mutual support, key to social and emotional well-being. Additionally, by normalizing differences and promoting kindness and inclusion, schools help create a safe

Fig. 3.2 The Mismatched Socks Day (example of an activity carried out at the primary school of Chignolo Po, Italy)

learning environment, reducing bullying and social exclusion. Finally, the initiative nurtures student agency, empowering them to take part in a school-wide culture of inclusivity. This sense of ownership boosts self-confidence and motivation, encouraging engagement in other community-building activities like peer mentoring, collaborative projects, and discussions on respect.

The impact of sense of community extends beyond students, and profoundly influences teachers' well-being, professional fulfilment, and overall job satisfaction. Educators who feel an integral part of their school community experience lower levels of stress, burnout, and emotional exhaustion, as a strong sense of community fosters emotional security, social belonging, and resilience. Teachers who perceive a deep connection with their school environment report greater job engagement, a stronger commitment to student success, and increased perseverance in managing classroom challenges (Collie et al., 2012). This impact of sense of community on teachers' well-being is further exemplified in personal testimonies from educators who recall their most fulfilling teaching experiences. One teacher, reflecting on her time in a particularly cohesive school, described the atmosphere as "a kind of family or even a vacation village, where we enjoyed our time with both students and colleagues. It never felt like work." This statement sums up the powerful role of a strong community in shaping teachers' perceptions of their professional experience. When educators feel emotionally connected to their school, the boundaries between professional obligations and personal fulfilment become blurred, allowing them to experience their role as deeply meaningful rather than merely a source of stress or exhaustion.

3.1.4 How Teacher-Student Relationships Shape Academic Achievement

High-quality teacher-student interactions play a crucial role in shaping students' academic achievement, particularly in the development of *literacy and numeracy skills*. The quality of these interactions is closely linked to language acquisition, preliteracy development, reading proficiency, and mathematical competence, with effects that extend well beyond early childhood education (Slot et al., 2018). The influence of emotionally supportive and instructional-rich teacher-student relationships is particularly pronounced in preschool and primary school, where foundational cognitive and academic skills are established. Evidence suggests that the impact of high-quality teacher-student interactions in kindergarten continues to be significant throughout later schooling years, with measurable effects persisting into sixth grade (Hofkens et al., 2023). Teachers who provide consistent emotional support and cognitively stimulating instruction create an environment conducive to learning, which enhances verbal skills, comprehension abilities, and overall literacy development. In early childhood education settings, instructional quality has been shown to foster vocabulary acquisition, phonological awareness, and emergent literacy skills, all of which are essential for later reading proficiency and academic success (Niklas & Tayler, 2018).

Furthermore, early exposure to rich language interactions with teachers plays a crucial role in strengthening semantic and syntactic knowledge, both of which are foundational to language development. Semantic knowledge refers to the understanding of word meanings, vocabulary, and the relationships between words, allowing children to comprehend and use language with precision and depth. In contrast, syntactic knowledge pertains to the rules governing sentence structure and grammar, enabling pupils to construct coherent, grammatically correct sentences and understand complex linguistic patterns (Nippold, 2016). These linguistic foundations are critical for developing advanced literacy skills and ensuring effective communication across academic domains. Beyond these, high-quality teacher-student language interactions also foster the development of expressive and receptive language abilities, which are essential for effective communication and academic engagement. Expressive language skills involve a child's ability to verbalize thoughts, convey ideas, and articulate messages clearly through both spoken and written language, facilitating participation in discussions and the ability to organize and communicate information effectively (Justice & Kaderavek, 2004). Receptive language skills, on the other hand, refer to the capacity to comprehend spoken and written language, interpret meaning accurately, and process complex verbal input, which is crucial for following instructions, understanding academic content, and engaging in meaningful conversations. Students with strong receptive language abilities tend to perform better in reading comprehension and problem-solving tasks, as they can decode, retain, and apply information more efficiently. Consequently, the mastery of these linguistic abilities enables students to actively participate in classroom discussions, respond appropriately to questions, follow multi-step instructions, and produce well-structured written compositions.

Research indicates that teachers' ability to foster a positive, encouraging, and emotionally secure classroom environment is directly correlated with students' *reading achievement*. In kindergarten, higher levels of teacher warmth, responsiveness, and encouragement have been linked to stronger reading skills in first grade, suggesting that emotional support plays a crucial role in sustaining early literacy development (Silinskas et al., 2017). Moreover, when teachers adopt individualized and responsive teaching approaches, students exhibit greater confidence in their reading abilities, higher levels of reading fluency, and improved comprehension skills.

Beyond language development and reading skills, teacher interaction quality also plays a critical role in *mathematical skill acquisition*. Research has demonstrated that high levels of instructional support contribute to the development of early numeracy concepts, arithmetic reasoning, and problem-solving abilities (Clements & Sarama, 2011). Children who experience structured mathematical discussions, guided problem-solving sessions, and explicit numerical instruction within an emotionally supportive environment demonstrate greater accuracy in number sense, better understanding of mathematical operations, and enhanced logical reasoning skills (Aunola et al., 2004). Furthermore, the combination of effective instructional techniques and a supportive classroom climate tends to reduce math anxiety, increase persistence in mathematical tasks, and strengthen overall engagement in learning numerical concepts.

3.1.5 Evaluating the Quality of Teacher-Student Relationships

According to Pianta (2001) teacher-student relationships can be described along three dimensions: *closeness*, *conflict*, and *dependency*. Closeness represents the affective component of the relationship, encompassing warmth, affection, open communication, emotional support, and engagement. A close relationship with a teacher allows students to develop positive attitudes towards school and academic demands, promotes their interest in participating in various activities, and facilitates effective communication. Teachers perceived as "close" to their students adopt a communicative style characterized by frequent and positive interactions within the classroom. These interactions enable students to view the teacher as a supportive figure they can turn to during moments of difficulty, fostering a sense of safety and trust. Conflict, on the other hand, refers to hostile behaviours or the absence of satisfactory relational interactions between the teacher and students. High levels of conflict can negatively impact academic performance, student participation, classroom climate, and the teacher's ability to manage behavioural problems effectively. This dimension poses a significant risk to the well-being of both students and teachers. Persistent conflict often leads to feelings of inefficacy and frustration on the teacher's part, while students experiencing such dynamics may disengage from the learning process and classroom interactions. Finally, dependency describes the degree to which a student relies on the teacher for support in completing any activity. Excessive dependency manifests as frequent requests for help, the need for physical proximity, heightened attention-seeking behaviours, and negative emotional reactions to moments of separation. While a certain degree of dependency is natural, excessive reliance on the teacher can hinder the development of student autonomy and social relationships. Such behaviours may isolate the student from peers, limiting opportunities to develop essential social skills necessary for integration into the classroom community.

The study of teacher-student relationships has led to the development of *observational* tools designed both to guide teachers' educational practices and to deepen the scientific analysis of relationship quality within the classroom. Among the most widely cited tools for assessing classroom relationships is the Classroom Assessment Scoring System (CLASS), developed by Pianta et al. (2008). CLASS is an observational instrument that allows for the systematic evaluation of the quality of teacher-student interactions. CLASS categorizes teacher-student interactions into three overarching domains namely *emotional support*, *classroom organization*, and *instructional support*. CLASS is designed for use by trained observers and can be applied across various educational levels, from early childhood education to upper secondary school. The CLASS framework structures observations into a 30-minute session, consisting of 20 minutes of classroom observation followed by 10 minutes of coding. Within each domain, specific dimensions are defined with observable and behavioural characteristics of teacher-child or child-child interactions, such as teacher sensitivity, behaviour management, and quality of feedback, which serve as key focal points for observation. These dimensions are rated on 1–7 scale, ranging from low to high. CLASS is intentionally designed to produce scores that capture broad, structured patterns of teacher behaviour while also offering specific, concrete examples that are valuable for both observers and practitioners (Table 3.1).

3.2 The Emotional Tapestry of Teacher-Student Bonds

Given the enduring impact of teacher-student relationships, this section presents a study examining how these experiences are embedded in the personal and professional memories of both in-service and pre-service teachers. By analysing both positive and negative recollections, the research explores the emotional significance of past interactions with teachers and their potential influence on educators' professional identity development. To investigate these dynamics, a qualitative study was conducted with 134 special pre-service and in-service teachers (103 female; M = 38.18 years, SD = 8.25; Min = 22, Max = 59), focusing on their remembered experiences with their own teachers during their schooling years.

Participants were asked to respond to two open-ended research questions: (1) "Can you recall a pleasant school-related episode involving your teachers? What happened?" and (2) "Can you recall an unpleasant school-related episode involving your teachers? What happened?" All responses were audio-recorded, transcribed verbatim, and analysed using thematic analysis (Braun & Clarke, 2006). Two independent researchers conducted the initial coding to capture diverse perspectives, identifying relevant data units (e.g., phrases or paragraphs) and categorizing them into potential themes based on similarities and differences. An iterative refinement process was undertaken to ensure coherence, with final validation by a third researcher to enhance reliability and accuracy.

To present the findings of this research, the following section, entitled "Nothing Compared to You: The Emotional Memories of Schooling", will outline the themes that emerged from the first research question,

Table 3.1 CLASS Framework for assessing quality in early childhood and elementary classrooms (adapted from Hofkens et al., 2023)

Domains	Dimensions
Emotional support This dimension assesses how teachers create a positive emotional climate, support students' social and emotional functioning, and foster warm and respectful interactions	• Positive climate: captures the general emotional atmosphere of the classroom and the relationship between teachers and students • Negative climate: indicates the overall level of negativity expressed in the classroom, including emotions such as anger, aggression, and irritability between teachers and students • Teacher sensitivity: represents teachers' responsiveness to students' needs and their awareness of students' academic and emotional well-being • Regard for student perspectives: the extent to which the teacher's interactions and classroom activities prioritize students' interests, motivations, and perspectives, rather than being predominantly teacher-centred
Classroom organization It evaluates teachers' ability to manage student behaviour, structure activities effectively, and promote an environment conducive to learning	• Behaviour management: reflects teachers' ability to implement effective strategies for preventing and managing misbehaviour by setting clear behavioural expectations and minimizing time spent addressing disciplinary issues • Productivity: evaluates how effectively teachers manage instructional time and classroom routines to maximize students' learning opportunities • Instructional learning formats: the extent to which teachers enhance students' engagement and learning by offering stimulating activities, effective instruction, interactive centres, and engaging materials • Classroom chaos: the extent to which teachers struggle to manage the classroom, resulting in frequent disruptions and a chaotic learning environment • Classroom management: the extent to which teachers establish clear instructions, rules, and routines that students understand while implementing well-timed proactive behavioural strategies instead of relying on control-based techniques. • Child responsibility: the degree to which teachers create opportunities for students to take on roles and work independently within the classroom.

(*continued*)

Table 3.1 (continued)

Domains	Dimensions
Instructional support It examines how teachers facilitate cognitive and language development through feedback, questioning techniques, and scaffolding strategies	• Concept development: the extent to which instructional discussions and activities encourage students' higher-order thinking skills rather than emphasizing rote memorization and fact-based learning • Quality of feedback: Evaluates the extent to which teachers provide feedback aimed at deepening students' learning and understanding (formative evaluation) rather than focusing solely on correctness or final outcomes (summative evaluation) • Language modelling: The quality and frequency of teachers' use of language stimulation and language-facilitation techniques during individual, small-group, and whole-class interactions with students • Instructional conversation: evaluates the extent to which teachers' verbal interactions with students are reciprocal and encourage reasoning, concept development, idea expression, and cognitive elaboration • Literacy instruction: the degree to which teachers engage students in reading activities, provide explicit phonics instruction, extend book discussions with comprehension and process questions, and expose students to written language • Richness of instructional methods: The degree to which teachers employ diverse strategies to enhance students' thinking and deepen their understanding of the material at a more complex level

which examined positive recollections of teacher-student relationships. Meanwhile, the section entitled, "Back to Black: The Darker Side of Teacher-Student Interactions", will focus on the themes identified in response to the second research question, which explored negative experiences in teacher-student relationships.

3.2.1 Nothing Compared to You: The Emotional Memories of Schooling

Thematic analysis identified seven main themes reflecting the diverse experiences, reflections, and emotions reported by teachers during the interviews.

Theme 1: Teacher empathy as a source of resilience. This theme captures instances in which teachers provided emotional support, helping students navigate difficult personal or academic situations. Rather than focusing solely on academic instruction, these teachers demonstrated attentiveness to students' well-being, offering reassurance and a sense of security. The emotional presence of educators allowed students to cope with stress, grief, or anxiety, fostering resilience and a more positive perception of school. One participant shared how a teacher's simple act of compassion made a significant difference during a difficult time: "During a period of family distress, my participation in school dropped. My teacher noticed and privately asked me what was happening. When I told her, I burst into tears, and she hugged me tightly, reassuring me and asking me to keep her updated. That moment gave me comfort and made me feel understood." Another described how a teacher's reaction to an anxiety-inducing exam situation helped them regain confidence: "I was about to be tested in front of the class when I completely froze. Instead of scolding me, my teacher gently told me to step outside, take a deep breath, and come back when I felt ready. This simple gesture turned a moment of panic into one of support, and I was able to continue the exam." These stories illustrate how teacher empathy, even in small moments, can provide students with emotional stability, helping them feel seen, valued, and capable of overcoming challenges. Teachers who demonstrated empathy and emotional awareness were instrumental in supporting students through personal difficulties. By recognizing their struggles and responding with understanding rather than judgment, these educators created a sense of security, helping students develop resilience and navigate both academic and personal challenges.

Theme 2: *Teachers as guides for passion and future aspirations.* Many students described how their teachers played a crucial role in shaping their academic interests and career trajectories. Through their enthusiasm, personalized encouragement, and deep commitment to their subjects, these teachers sparked new passions or reinforced existing ones, leaving a lasting impact on students' futures. An example of this can be found in a participant who initially disliked playing the guitar but changed their perspective due to their teacher's passion: "At first, I hated playing the guitar. However, my music teacher's enthusiasm and passion for teaching gradually made me appreciate music. His influence shaped my lifelong approach to musical learning." Similarly, another one recounted how a simple act of kindness from a philosophy professor influenced their academic path: "My philosophy professor sent me a condolence message after my father's passing. This small act of kindness made me feel valued beyond being just a student. It also played a role in my decision to study philosophy at university." These narratives highlight how teachers, through their engagement and personal connection with students, became central figures in fostering intellectual curiosity and guiding students towards meaningful educational and career choices.

Theme 3: *Personalized academic support and recognition of potential.* This theme focuses on how individualized attention from teachers enabled students to overcome academic challenges and recognize their own potential. Some students struggled with certain subjects or doubted their abilities, but teachers who provided tailored support helped them persist and build confidence in their skills. Teachers who provided individualized support helped students overcome academic challenges and recognize their own capabilities. By adapting their approach, offering encouragement, or simply acknowledging effort, these educators played a crucial role in fostering students' confidence and persistence. One participant recalled how a professor's patience transformed their academic experience: "I struggled with a topic in physiology, so I scheduled a meeting with my professor. She patiently explained it multiple times until I fully understood. That moment made me feel supported and capable, and her passion for the subject ultimately inspired me to write my thesis in physiology." Another student described how a teacher's belief in their abilities changed their academic trajectory: "I was failing Latin and had already started looking into transferring to another school. When my teacher found out, she asked to meet with me. She reassured me that my difficulties were temporary and that I had the potential to succeed. Thanks to that conversation, I stayed, and in the end, I did well in Latin." These examples highlight how tailored support and encouragement from teachers can be important in shaping students' self-perception, helping them persist through challenges and reach their academic goals.

Theme 4: *The classroom as a community for emotional expression and connection.* This theme highlights how certain teachers fostered a sense of belonging and emotional connection among students. By creating structured activities that encouraged self-expression and empathy, these teachers contributed to a more cohesive and supportive classroom environment. Some teachers went beyond traditional instruction to create spaces where students could express emotions, reflect on their experiences, and develop deeper connections with their peers. These educators actively fostered a sense of belonging, making the classroom a place for both academic and personal growth. One participant recalled a particular initiative by their teacher: "Our social sciences teacher created a space called the 'thinking corner,' where we wrote emotional diaries and later shared our reflections. Reading others' stories helped us understand different perspectives and strengthened our sense of belonging." Another described how a classroom discussion, prompted by a classmate's difficult experience, became an opportunity for emotional engagement: "A classmate shared an experience of mistreatment at the boarding school where he lived. Our teacher welcomed his story, allowing him to reflect on his feelings of guilt while giving all of us the chance to express our own thoughts. That moment made me realize that school wasn't just about academics but also about listening and sharing." By incorporating these approaches, teachers transformed their classrooms into communities of mutual understanding, reinforcing students' emotional and social development alongside their academic progress.

Theme 5: *The long-term impact of small gestures of care.* This theme focuses on how seemingly small but meaningful actions from teachers had a profound and lasting impact on students' perception of school and relationships with educators. Acts of kindness, such as checking in on a student's well-being, sending letters, or recognizing achievements, left an enduring emotional imprint. Seemingly small acts of kindness from teachers had a profound and lasting effect on students, shaping their perception of school as a place of support and emotional connection. Whether through simple check-ins, personal recognition, or thoughtful gestures, these moments reinforced students' sense of value and belonging. One person reflected on a childhood memory that remained vivid decades later: "When I was home sick for a long period, my primary school teacher visited me, bringing a small gift. Forty years later, she still remembers my name. That simple act made me feel seen and cared for in a way I never forgot." Another student described how a handwritten letter from a teacher during an absence provided unexpected comfort: "Whenever we missed school due to illness, our teacher would send us a letter through a classmate, asking how we were and reminding us not to worry about catching up. I kept those letters for years, and they always reminded me of how much she cared." These stories show how even the smallest gestures of attention and care from educators can leave a lasting imprint, reinforcing students' trust in their teachers and shaping their emotional connection to the learning environment.

Theme 6: Teacher advocacy in overcoming institutional barriers. This theme explores cases in which teachers actively advocated for students, helping them navigate bureaucratic or parental constraints to access important educational opportunities. Teachers in these narratives went beyond their traditional roles to ensure students received the support they needed. In several cases, teachers played a crucial role in advocating for students, ensuring they had access to opportunities that external circumstances or institutional policies initially denied them. These educators actively intervened on behalf of their students, demonstrating a commitment that extended beyond the classroom. One participant shared how their teacher personally engaged with their parents to secure an important academic opportunity: "My German teacher personally spoke to my parents, persuading them to allow me to participate in a student exchange in Germany. That experience changed my life and ultimately led me to pursue a thesis in German studies." Another student described how a professor fought against bureaucratic restrictions to help them gain valuable work experience: "I had the opportunity to complete my internship at a company, but the school initially denied it because internships could not be activated at that time of the year. However, my teacher personally intervened, negotiating with the school administration and the company hosting me to ensure I could participate. Knowing that she believed in me and fought for my right to receive training was incredibly meaningful to me." These instances highlight how teachers, through their advocacy and dedication, were instrumental in ensuring that students had access to meaningful experiences that shaped their academic and personal development.

Theme 7: *The role of playfulness and creativity in learning.* This theme highlights the impact of teachers who integrated humour, creativity, and unconventional teaching methods into their instruction. Such approaches not only made learning more engaging but also reshaped students' perceptions of teachers as approachable figures. Some teachers broke away from rigid instructional methods, incorporating humour, creativity, and unconventional approaches to engage students and make learning more enjoyable. These moments alleviated academic pressure and strengthened students' connection with their teachers. One student recalled how a light-hearted classroom prank left a lasting impression: "On April Fools' Day, our math teacher gave the boys a fake surprise test while secretly informing the girls it was a joke. He kept up the act until the very end, watching the boys panic before revealing the prank. It was one of the funniest moments of our school years, and it showed us that our teacher saw us as more than just students—he wanted us to have fun too." Another participant remembered an emotional moment during a school trip: "At the end of our school trip, our teachers gathered with us in the hotel lobby for a final reflection. For the first time, we saw them not just as authority figures but as people who genuinely cared about us. Some even teared up as we talked about our experiences. That moment made me feel incredibly close to them." These experiences highlight how humour and human connection can transform traditional student-teacher dynamics, making the learning environment more engaging and emotionally enriching.

The emotions reported by participants in these narratives include a broad spectrum of positive affective responses to meaningful school experiences, ranging from deep gratitude and admiration to feelings of empowerment, confidence, and belonging.

Many participants described experiencing a profound sense of appreciation for teachers who demonstrated empathy and personal investment in their well-being. One student recalled, "During my first day of school, I was extremely nervous. The teacher took my hand, smiled at me, and walked me to class. That small gesture immediately reassured me and set the tone for the warm and caring relationship we would share throughout my primary school years." This expression of security and emotional comfort was echoed in several accounts where teachers provided direct support in moments of distress. Feelings of pride and self-confidence emerged prominently in narratives where educators acknowledged and valued students' efforts and talents. One student shared: "I was in my final year of primary school when my teacher took one of my drawings and showed it to the entire class. I felt incredibly proud in that moment." Another participant recounted the validation that came from public recognition: "When I was 12, my essay was selected to be read aloud during the Holocaust Remembrance Day event. It made me feel proud and significantly boosted my self-confidence." Such moments of positive reinforcement were frequently linked to an increased sense of self-efficacy and motivation to continue excelling.

Several participants reported experiencing deep admiration and respect for teachers who transcended their instructional roles to form meaningful connections with students. This admiration was often tied to the recognition of teachers as figures of inspiration. One student recalled the impact of a philosophy professor's passion: "His dedication and knowledge captivated us so much that every lecture ended with an applause, and I left the classroom feeling inspired and intellectually fulfilled." Such enthusiasm of teachers not only heightened engagement with the subject matter but also shaped long-term academic and career aspirations. The feeling of belonging was another crucial emotional response, particularly in cases where teachers fostered inclusive and supportive classroom environments. For instance, participation in extracurricular activities, such as collaborative film projects or academic competitions, strengthened students' group identity. One student reflected, "During a mathematics competition, our teacher wasn't just a supervisor—he was cheering for us like a coach. It was the first time I truly felt part of a team." Finally, participants often described feelings of relief and encouragement when teachers showed flexibility and understanding regarding academic performance. Many recalled instances where educators accommodated students' needs, such as postponing assessments to reduce stress. One student noted, "Our Latin teacher frequently rescheduled tests if we had multiple exams on the same day. Knowing she cared about our workload made me feel more motivated and supported in my studies."

These narratives together illustrate how positive school experiences are deeply intertwined with emotions of security, appreciation, confidence, admiration, and belonging. When teachers engage with students on a personal level, recognizing their individual needs, aspirations, and struggles, they create an educational environment that fosters not only academic achievement but also long-term emotional well-being.

3.3 From Protectors to Perpetrators

While positive interactions foster academic engagement, emotional security, and a supportive learning environment, deteriorated or conflictual relationships can have severe consequences for both students and educators. Extensive research has examined the implications of negative student-teacher interactions, particularly concerning students' psychological and academic outcomes. Within this framework, growing attention has been directed towards the phenomenon of *teacher bullying*, which encompasses repeated harmful behaviours by teachers towards students, characterized by a power imbalance (Gusfre et al., 2024). This form of bullying includes both direct actions, such as physical aggression, and indirect forms of psychological violence, including verbal insults, humiliation, and social exclusion. Defined as a sustained pattern of negative behaviours aimed at exerting control or dominance over students, teacher bullying has been increasingly recognized as a critical issue with far-reaching consequences not only for student well-being and the broader school climate but also for teachers themselves.

Traditionally, bullying research has focused on student roles (e.g., bully, victim, bystander). However, emerging studies indicate that some teachers not only overlook bullying but actively engage in it, leveraging their authority to exert control over students. This phenomenon, known as "role-switching", occurs when educators shift from being protectors to aggressors, using relational aggression in public settings to reinforce hierarchical power structures (Gumpel et al., 2014). While such behaviours are often framed as disciplinary actions, evidence suggests that practices like public humiliation and negative reinforcement can intensify student marginalization, fostering feelings of isolation and psychological distress.

More specifically, research suggests that teachers who engage in bullying often target students perceived as challenging, disruptive, or socially marginalized (Gusfre et al., 2023). This behaviour has severe consequences for students, including increased levels of anxiety, depression, and academic disengagement (Modin et al., 2015). Additionally, students who experience bullying from teachers face an increased risk of peer victimization. Those who report being bullied by teachers are significantly more likely to become targets of peer aggression, reinforcing a cascading effect in which negative teacher-student interactions contribute to the normalization and perpetuation of bullying within the school environment.

Engaging in such behaviours has profound implications for teachers' mental health, often resulting in heightened stress, emotional exhaustion, and a growing sense of professional dissatisfaction. Several factors contribute to the emergence of bullying behaviours among teachers, many of which are rooted in occupational stress and the broader school environment. High levels of job-related pressure, excessive workloads, and burnout have been identified as significant risk factors (Khoury-Kassabri, 2009; Yen et al., 2015). When teachers perceive inadequate institutional support, lack of administrative guidance, or an overwhelming number of professional responsibilities, they may experience frustration and emotional dysregulation, which can sometimes be displaced onto students. Teachers who struggle with self-regulation and report low job satisfaction are particularly prone to engaging in negative interactions with students, further exacerbating an already strained classroom dynamic.

The organizational climate within schools also plays a crucial role in shaping teacher behaviour. Schools that lack clear disciplinary policies or maintain a permissive stance towards aggressive behaviours tend to report higher instances of teacher bullying. Unclear authority structures and inconsistent enforcement of behavioural expectations create environments where teachers, faced with ongoing classroom mismanagement and student misconduct, may resort to controlling and punitive measures to assert authority. Ambiguous authority structures can manifest in schools where disciplinary responsibilities are not clearly defined, leaving teachers uncertain about their role in managing student behaviour. For instance, when school policies fail to specify whether classroom discipline falls under the jurisdiction of individual teachers or administrative staff, educators may feel unsupported and compelled to handle misbehaviour independently, often through harsh disciplinary tactics. Similarly, inconsistent enforcement of behavioural expectations occurs when school leadership applies disciplinary measures unevenly, allowing some students to evade consequences while others face excessive punishment. A lack of standardized responses to disruptive behaviour, such as frequent leniency towards repeat offenders or conflicting disciplinary guidelines from different administrators, can foster frustration among teachers, leading them to adopt stricter, more authoritarian approaches. In such highly challenging environments, teachers may adopt bullying as a maladaptive coping strategy – namely dysfunctional behavioural and emotional responses used to manage stress that, rather than alleviating distress, tend to reinforce negative patterns and contribute to further emotional and psychological strain. In this context, teachers may employ aggression, intimidation, or exclusion as mechanisms to regain a sense of control. However, rather than mitigating classroom difficulties, these behaviours tend to perpetuate cycles of hostility, disengagement, and further disciplinary issues, ultimately undermining both teacher and student well-being.

3.3.1 Back to Black: The Darker Side of Teacher-Student Interactions

Building on the previously cited literature, this section presents the thematic analysis conducted on qualitative data exploring teachers' recollections of negative experiences in teacher-student relationships during their schooling years. The analysis identified six key themes, reflecting the diverse perspectives, insights, and emotions expressed by teachers during the interviews.

Theme 1: *The psychological impact of humiliation and verbal abuse.* Several narratives illustrate the lasting emotional damage caused by teachers' humiliating remarks or verbal abuse. These experiences often led to diminished self-esteem, anxiety, and, in some cases, long-term aversion to certain subjects or learning environments. A clear example of this appears in one student's recollection: "When I was nine, my teacher asked us to write about what we wanted to be when we grew up. I wrote that I wanted to be a surgeon. When she checked our work, she smirked sarcastically at my spelling mistake and made it clear I would never achieve that dream. I removed medicine from my career choices entirely, likely because of that moment." Another participant described a similarly distressing event: "During a surprise oral test, I gave an incorrect answer, and the teacher told me, 'Well, Marta, with that answer, you might as well throw yourself out the window.' I felt deeply humiliated and devastated." These examples highlight how derogatory comments from educators, whether about intelligence, aspirations, or performance, can have profound and lasting consequences on students' confidence and self-perception.

Theme 2: *The effects of unjustified punishment and authoritarianism.* Many students reported experiences where teachers exercised rigid control, implementing harsh punishments that instilled fear rather than discipline. In these cases, students felt powerless and unfairly treated, which led to negative associations with school and learning. One student recalled how an elementary school teacher physically disciplined a classmate: "My math teacher would openly tell us to avoid weaker students, calling them 'inferior.' One day, she forced a struggling boy to remove his shoes in front of the class, humiliating him for his 'bad smell.' We were all mortified, not just for him but for the sheer cruelty of the moment." Another described an experience of public embarrassment: "At the end of a dictation exercise, my teacher suddenly tore pages out of my notebook in front of the class because I hadn't followed her instructions perfectly. The overwhelming feeling of inadequacy crushed me in an instant." These stories suggest that excessive authoritarianism and punitive approaches can lead to feelings of fear, helplessness, and deep-seated resentment towards school.

Theme 3: *Gender-based and social discrimination by teachers.* Some narratives indicate that teachers treated students differently based on gender or socioeconomic background, reinforcing stereotypes and contributing to feelings of exclusion and injustice. One person recalled a teacher's bias against female students: "My philosophy teacher clearly disliked girls. She never called on the boys for questioning, while the girls were constantly interrogated and humiliated. I remember one instance where she told my classmate, 'I know you try, poor thing, but you just can't get it.' My classmate left the classroom in tears, and I developed a strong aversion to the subject." Another student described how a teacher used language to belittle their social background: "In third grade, I used the word 'mentina' instead of 'mint candy' in a writing exercise. My teacher seized on this minor dialectal difference as an opportunity to mock my family's social status in front of the entire class. Since then, I have struggled with public speaking, always fearing judgment." These incidents reveal how biased attitudes in educators can reinforce social divisions and shape students' perceptions of their own worth and abilities.

Theme 4: *The long-term impact of unwarranted academic discouragement.* Some students described how teachers actively discouraged them from pursuing academic goals, leading to self-doubt and lost opportunities. When educators dismiss students' potential, these negative messages often shape their self-perception well into adulthood. One person shared his experience with a discouraging teacher: "During my parent-teacher meeting, my literature professor told my parents I had chosen the wrong school and should have gone to a vocational institute. When I later submitted a written assignment, I was proud of, she accused me of having my father write it for me." Another one described a persistent pattern of being told they were not suited for a subject: "My pedagogy professor constantly gave me failing grades, insisting that this subject wasn't for me. For years, I believed I wasn't capable of understanding pedagogy, despite my passion for it." These experiences clarify how the subjects internalize negative feedback, sometimes abandoning aspirations altogether due to repeated discouragement.

Theme 5: *Lack of empathy and support during personal hardships.* Some participants recounted moments when teachers displayed an alarming lack of empathy during times of personal crisis, making them feel isolated and unsupported. One person described the absence of compassion from teachers during a personal loss: "Just before my final exams, I lost my father to cancer. The teachers showed no concern for my grief, focusing only on my performance. Looking back, I am proud that I chose to spend time with my father instead of dedicating every moment to studying. A parent's life is worth more than a grade." Another describes how a teacher disregarded a student's medical condition: "I suffered from a urinary tract condition, so I urgently asked my teacher to use the restroom. Even though she knew about my condition, she refused. I couldn't hold it and ended up wetting myself in class. The bullying from my classmates that followed isolated me for years." These narratives emphasize how a lack of teacher empathy during crucial moments can deepen student distress and create lasting psychological scars.

Theme 6: *Physical and personal boundary violations by teachers.* Several narratives revealed incidents where teachers crossed physical or personal boundaries, making students feel unsafe in the classroom. One person described an incident with their math teacher: "I was at the blackboard solving a problem when the teacher suddenly tried to spank me as a joke. I immediately reacted, threatening to report him. My classmates were shocked, and from that day on, I lost all motivation to study mathematics." Another shared how a physical education teacher acted without consent: "While performing a somersault, I cut my head on my hair clip. Without asking for my permission, my physical education teacher simply cut off part of my hair to disinfect the wound. I felt completely disregarded, as if my opinion didn't matter at all." These experiences highlight the importance of respecting students' boundaries and ensuring that teachers act in ways that promote trust and security.

These narratives reveal a complex range of emotions experienced by participants, often deeply ingrained due to the distressing nature of their school experiences. Feelings of humiliation and shame were among the most frequently reported, particularly in response to public embarrassment inflicted by teachers. One participant recalled, "During an English test, the teacher accused me of cheating in front of the whole class and forced me to retake the exam sitting next to her desk. I felt deeply ashamed as if all my efforts had been erased in a single moment." This sense of humiliation was frequently accompanied by frustration, especially when students perceived the situation as unjust. Another participant described, "I had put so much effort into preparing my assignment, but the teacher dismissed it entirely, claiming it was beyond my capabilities. It was infuriating to know that no matter how much effort I put in, my work would never be recognized." Fear and anxiety emerged as dominant emotions, particularly concerning teachers who used intimidation as a disciplinary method. One person recounted, "Every time the teacher walked into the room, I felt my stomach tighten, knowing that someone would be singled out and humiliated. I lived in constant dread of being the next target." The unpredictability of verbal attacks and punitive measures often resulted in long-term emotional distress.

Powerlessness was another recurring emotional response, as participants frequently felt incapable of reacting or defending themselves in an environment where the teacher's authority was absolute. One expressed this feeling vividly: "When the teacher told my parents that I was not suited for academic studies, I felt completely powerless. No matter what I said or did, the decision had already been made for me." Betrayal and disappointment surfaced in cases where students expected fairness and support but instead encountered indifference or mistreatment. This was particularly evident in situations involving a lack of empathy. One person shared, "I was grieving the loss of a family member, and not a single teacher acknowledged my pain. They only cared about my grades, which made me feel like I was nothing more than a number." In contrast, anger was often reported in response to overtly discriminatory or degrading treatment, particularly in instances of bias. One participant, reflecting on gender-based discrimination, stated, "It was infuriating to see the boys in my class receiving good grades without ever being questioned, while we girls were scrutinized and humiliated at every opportunity." Finally, sadness and a profound sense of inadequacy were commonly associated with long-term academic discouragement. Many participants internalized negative feedback, leading to persistent self-doubt. One person described this emotional burden, saying, "After years of hearing that I wasn't intelligent enough, I started to believe it. Even now, when I face a challenge, that voice is still there, telling me I am not capable." These emotions, often intertwined and overlapping, highlight the enduring psychological impact of negative educational experiences, shaping students' self-perception and emotional well-being far beyond the classroom setting.

3.4 Rethinking Teacher-Student Relationships in Educational Research and Practice

The narratives and empirical evidence presented in this chapter underscore the profound and lasting impact that teacher-student relationships can have on students' academic trajectories, psychological well-being, and self-perception. While positive interactions serve as a foundation for engagement, emotional security, and learning, conflictual or harmful teacher behaviours can lead to deep-seated distress, reinforcing cycles of exclusion, self-doubt, and disengagement (Modin et al., 2015).

A crucial implication of these findings is the need to expand the conceptualization of teacher responsibility beyond curriculum delivery to encompass the relational and emotional dimensions of teaching. Teachers who engage in relational aggression often do so not out of inherent malevolence but as a maladaptive coping mechanism for occupational stress, burnout, and institutional neglect. Addressing this issue requires a paradigm shift in teacher training, expanding the focus beyond the technical aspects of instruction to integrate evidence-based strategies that support teachers' emotional and relational competencies. This encompasses emotional regulation strategies that enable educators to effectively manage stress and cope successfully challenging classroom situations, as well as training in relational ethics, which provides a framework for teacher-student interactions grounded in respect, fairness, and the responsible use of authority. Relational ethics emphasize the importance of cultivating a trust-based, inclusive, and non-coercive learning environment, where teachers remain aware of power dynamics and intentionally foster interactions that uphold students' dignity, autonomy, and sense of belonging (Walker, 2015).

At a broader level, these findings highlight the systemic nature of relational dynamics in schools. The presence of teacher bullying is not simply an issue of individual misconduct but reflects institutional climates that permit or overlook relational aggression (Gumpel et al., 2014). Schools that lack clear ethical guidelines, structured support for teachers, and well-defined disciplinary policies create environments where coercive and punitive behaviours can flourish unchecked. Future research should focus on developing multi-level intervention models, integrating teacher mental health support, peer accountability structures, and student advocacy mechanisms to ensure that relational well-being is prioritized within school policies.

Finally, rethinking the ethical and emotional dimensions of teacher-student relationships is not just a moral imperative but a scientific necessity. By adopting a holistic, evidence-based, and systemically informed perspective, education can move towards a future in which schools are not just sites of knowledge transmission but spaces of psychological safety, empowerment, and human connection.

References

Antognazza, D. (2017). *Crescere emotivamente competenti. Come sviluppare le competenze socio-emotive a scuola [Grow emotionally competent. How to develop social-emotional skills at school]*. La Meridiana.

Arens, A. K., & Morin, A. J. S. (2016). Relations between teachers' emotional exhaustion and students' educational outcomes. *Journal of Educational Psychology, 108*(6), 800–813. https://doi.org/10.1037/edu0000105

Aunola, K., Leskinen, E., Lerkkanen, M.-K., & Nurmi, J.-E. (2004). Developmental dynamics of math performance from preschool to grade 2. *Journal of Educational Psychology, 96*(4), 699–713. https://doi.org/10.1037/0022-0663.96.4.699

Baumeister, R. F., & Vohs, K. D. (Eds.). (2004). *Handbook of self-regulation: Research, theory, and applications*. The Guilford Press.

Bodrova, E., & Leong, D. J. (2006). The development of self-regulation in young children: Implications for teacher training. In M. Zaslow & I. Martinez-Beck (Eds.), *Future directions in teacher training* (pp. 203–224). Brooks-Cole.

Braun, V., & Clarke, V. (2006). Using thematic analysis in psychology. *Qualitative Research in Psychology, 3*(2), 77–101. https://doi.org/10.1191/1478088706qp063o

Cadima, J., Verschueren, K., Leal, T., & Guedes, C. (2016). Classroom interactions, dyadic teacher–child relationships, and self–regulation in socially disadvantaged young children. *Journal of Abnormal Child Psychology, 44*(1), 7–17. https://doi.org/10.1007/s10802-015-0060-5

Cavioni, V., & Grazzani, I. (2023). *L'apprendimento sociale ed emotivo: Teorie e buone pratiche per promuovere la salute mentale a scuola [Social and emotional learning: Theories and best practices for promoting mental health at school]*. Il Mulino.

Cavioni, V., & Toto, G. (2024). Exploring pre-service special education teachers' self-perceptions in addressing students' academic, social, and emotional needs. In C. Cefai (Ed.), *Nurturing the wellbeing of students in difficulty. The Legacy of Paul Cooper* (pp. 85–107). Peter Lang.

Cavioni, V., Grazzani, V., Ornaghi, V., Agliati, A., & Pepe, A. (2021). Adolescents' mental health at school: The mediating role of life satisfaction. *Frontiers in Psychology, 12*, 720628. https://doi.org/10.3389/fpsyg.2021.720628

Clements, D. H., & Sarama, J. (2011). Early childhood mathematics intervention. *Science, 333*(6045), 968–970. https://doi.org/10.1126/science.1204537

Collie, R. J., Shapka, J. D., & Perry, N. E. (2012). School climate and social-emotional learning: Predicting teacher stress, job satisfaction, and teaching efficacy. *Journal of Educational Psychology, 104*(4), 1189–1204. https://doi.org/10.1037/a0029356

Endedijk, H. M., Breeman, L. D., van Lissa, C. J., Hendrickx, M. M. H. G., den Boer, L., & Mainhard, T. (2022). The Teacher's invisible hand: A meta-analysis of the relevance of teacher-student relationship quality for peer relationships and the contribution of student behavior. *Review of Educational Research, 92*(3), 370–412. https://doi.org/10.3102/00346543211051428

Farmer, T. W., McAuliffe Lines, M., & Hamm, J. V. (2011). Revealing the invisible hand: The role of teachers in children's peer experiences. *Journal of Applied Developmental Psychology, 32*(5), 247–256. https://doi.org/10.1016/j.appdev.2011.04.006

Gasser, L., Grütter, J., Buholzer, A., & Wettstein, A. (2018). Emotionally supportive classroom interactions and students' perceptions of their teachers as caring and just. *Learning and Instruction, 54*, 82–92. https://doi.org/10.1016/j.learninstruc.2017.08.003

Grayson, J. L., & Alvarez, H. K. (2008). School climate factors relating to teacher burnout: A mediator model. *Teaching and Teacher Education, 24*(5), 1349–1363. https://doi.org/10.1016/j.tate.2007.06.005

Gumpel, T. P., Zioni-Koren, V., & Bekerman, Z. (2014). An ethnographic study of participant roles in school bullying. *Aggressive Behavior, 40*(3), 214–228. https://doi.org/10.1002/ab.21515

Gusfre, K. S., Støen, J., & Fandrem, H. (2023). Bullying by teachers towards students—A scoping review. *International Journal of Bullying Prevention, 5*, 331–347. https://doi.org/10.1007/s42380-022-00131-z

Gusfre, K. S., Yanagida, T., Støen, J., & Fandrem, H. (2024). Teacher bullying—Does it have an impact on peer bullying victimization? *International Journal of Bullying Prevention*. https://doi.org/10.1007/s42380-024-00273-2

Hamre, B., Hatfield, B., Pianta, R., & Jamil, F. (2013). Evidence for general and domain-specific elements of teacher-child interactions: Associations with preschool children's development. *Child Development, 85*(3), 1257–1274. https://doi.org/10.1111/cdev.12184

Hofkens, T., Pianta, R. C., & Hamre, B. (2023). Teacher-student interactions: Theory, measurement, and evidence for universal properties that support students' learning across countries and cultures. In R. Maulana, M. Helms-Lorenz, & R. M. Klassen (Eds.), *Effective teaching around the world*. Springer.

Hughes, J. N., Luo, W., Kwok, O. M., & Loyd, L. K. (2008). Teacher–student support, effortful engagement, and achievement: A 3-year longitudinal study. *Journal of Educational Psychology, 100*(1), 1–14. https://doi.org/10.1037/0022-0663.100.1.1

Justice, L. M., & Kaderavek, J. N. (2004). Embedded-explicit emergent literacy intervention I: Background and description of approach. *Language, Speech, and Hearing Services in Schools, 35*(3), 201–211. https://doi.org/10.1044/0161-1461(2004/020)

Khoury-Kassabri, M. (2009). The relationship between staff maltreatment of students and bully-victim group membership. *Child Abuse & Neglect, 33*(12), 914–923. https://doi.org/10.1016/j.chiabu.2009.05.005

Maldonado-Carreño, C., & Votruba-Drzal, E. (2011). Teacher-child relationships and the development of academic and behavioral skills during elementary school: A within- and between-child analysis. *Child Development, 82*(2), 601–616. https://doi.org/10.1111/j.1467-8624.2010.01533.x

Modin, B., Låftman, S. B., & Östberg, V. (2015). Bullying in context: An analysis of psychosomatic complaints among adolescents in Stockholm. *Journal of School Violence, 14*(4), 382–404. https://doi.org/10.1080/15388220.2014.928640

Murray, C., & Greenberg, M. T. (2000). Children's relationship with teachers and bonds with school and investigation of patterns and correlates in middle childhood. *Journal of School Psychology, 38*(5), 423–445. https://doi.org/10.1016/S0022-4405(00)00034-0

Niklas, F., & Tayler, C. (2018). Room quality and composition matters: Children's verbal and numeracy abilities in Australian early childhood settings. *Learning and Instruction, 54*, 114–124. https://doi.org/10.1016/j.learninstruc.2017.08.006

Nippold, M. A. (2016). *Later language development: School-age children, adolescents, and young adults* (4th ed.). Pro-Ed.

O'Connor, E. E., Dearing, E., & Collins, B. A. (2011). Teacher-child relationship and behavior problem trajectories in elementary school. *American Educational Research Journal, 48*(1), 120–162. https://doi.org/10.3102/0002831210365008

Ocak, S. (2010). The effects of child-teacher relationships on interpersonal problem-solving skills of children. *Infants & Young Children, 23*(4), 312–322.

Pakarinen, E., Aunola, K., Kiuru, N., Lerkkanen, M. K., Poikkeus, A. M., Siekkinen, M., & Nurmi, J. E. (2014). The cross-lagged associations between classroom interactions and children's achievement behaviors. *Contemporary Educational Psychology, 39*(3), 248–261. https://doi.org/10.1016/j.cedpsych.2014.06.001

Pianta, R. C. (2001). *Student-teacher relationship scale: Professional manual.* Psychological Assessment Resources, Inc.

Pianta, R. C., Hamre, B., & Stuhlman, M. (2003). Relationships between teachers and children. In W. M. Reynolds & G. E. Miller (Eds.), *Comprehensive handbook of psychology* (Vol. 7, pp. 199–234). John Wiley & Sons, Inc.

Pianta, R. C., La Paro, K. M., & Hamre, B. K. (2008). *Classroom assessment scoring system (CLASS) manual, Pre-K.* Paul H. Brookes Pub. Co.

Pöysä, S., Vasalampi, K., Muotka, J., Lerkkanen, M. K., Poikkeus, A. M., & Nurmi, J. E. (2019). Teacher–student interaction and lower secondary school students' situational engagement. *British Journal of Educational Psychology, 89*(2), 374–392. https://doi.org/10.1111/bjep.1224

Sabol, T. J., Hong, S. S., Pianta, R. C., & Burchinal, M. R. (2013). Can rating pre-k programs predict children's learning? *Science, 341*(6148), 845–846. https://doi.org/10.1126/science.1233

Silinskas, G., Pakarinen, E., Lerkkanen, M. K., Poikkeus, A. M., & Nurmi, J. E. (2017). Classroom interaction and literacy activities in kindergarten: Longitudinal links to grade 1 readers at risk and not at risk of reading difficulties. *Contemporary Educational Psychology, 51*, 321–335. https://doi.org/10.1016/j.cedpsych.2017.09.002

Slot, P. L., Bleses, D., Justice, L. M., Markussen-Brown, J., & Højen, A. (2018). Structural and process quality of Danish preschools: Direct and indirect associations with children's growth in language and preliteracy skills. *Early Education and Development, 29*(4), 581–602. https://doi.org/10.1080/10409289.2018.1452494

Spilt, J. L., Koomen, H. M. Y., & Thijs, J. T. (2011). Teacher wellbeing: The importance of teacher–student relationships. *Educational Psychology Review, 23*(4), 457–477. https://doi.org/10.1007/s10648-011-9170-y

Walker, S. (2015). Relationship-based teaching: A relational ethics led approach to teaching social work. *Ethics and Social Welfare, 9*(4), 394–402. https://doi.org/10.1080/17496535.2015.1088703

Wentzel, K. R. (2015). Socialization in school settings. In J. E. Grusec & P. D. Hastings (Eds.), *Handbook of socialization: Theory and research* (2nd ed., pp. 251–275). The Guilford Press.

Williford, A., Whittaker, J., Vitiello, J., & Downer, J. (2013). Children's engagement within the preschool classroom and their development of self-regulation. *Early Education and Development, 24*, 162–187. https://doi.org/10.1080/10409289.2011.628270

Yen, C.-F., Ko, C.-H., Liu, T.-L., & Hu, H.-F. (2015). Physical child abuse and teacher harassment and their effects on mental health problems amongst adolescent bully-victims in Taiwan. *Child Psychiatry & Human Development, 46*(5), 683–692. https://doi.org/10.1007/s10578-014-0510-2

4

Advancing Teacher Mental Health: Case Studies of Good Practice

Abstract This chapter examines the implementation and impact of two European programmes—Promoting Mental Health at Schools (PROMEHS) and Teaching to Be (T2Be)—designed to enhance teacher well-being and social-emotional competence. While school-based interventions on teacher mental health have traditionally focused on reducing stress and burnout, the whole-school approach has gained increasing recognition as a more sustainable framework for integrating mental health promotion into education. The chapter underscores the importance of embedding teacher well-being initiatives within broader educational policies, ensuring sustainability and systemic impact.

Keywords School-based programme • Mental health literacy • Teachers' training • PROMEHS • T2Be • Gamification

V. Cavioni, *Fostering Teachers' Mental Health*,
https://doi.org/10.1007/978-3-031-92571-9_4

4.1 Empowering Educators: Key Components for Effective School Interventions

School-based interventions addressing teacher mental health have largely been developed in response to concerns related to stress and burnout, focusing on strategies such as mindfulness, relaxation techniques, and emotional self-regulation. Programmes such as Cultivating Awareness and Resilience in Education (CARE for Teachers) have been identified as effective in reducing psychological distress, improving emotional regulation, and enhancing teacher-student interactions (Jennings et al., 2017). Similarly, initiatives such as Building Educators' Skills in Adolescent Mental Health (BEAM) have been designed to improve teachers' ability to recognize and respond to students' psychological difficulties (Parker et al., 2021).

Given the complexity of mental health promotion in schools, the whole-school approach has been widely advocated in the literature as an essential framework for sustainable and systemic change (Cefai et al., 2021; Weare & Nind, 2011). This approach emphasizes the need for a multi-level intervention strategy that integrates mental health promotion into all aspects of school life, engaging students, teachers, parents, and school leadership in a collaborative effort. A core principle of this approach is that schools cannot effectively promote student well-being without first addressing the mental health needs of teachers (Cavioni & Grazzani, 2023; Cefai & Cavioni, 2014). As such, mental health initiatives should not only focus on equipping teachers with skills to support students but also ensure that teachers themselves develop social and emotional competences, and a strong sense of professional well-being. To establish schools as effective promoters of mental health, interventions must incorporate specific features that address both teachers' well-being and their capacity to support students. Below, specific key components necessary to ensure that schools become environments conducive to mental health promotion are outlined.

Prioritizing teacher mental health and risk management strategies. Given the substantial emotional demands of teaching, educators need effective tools for self-regulation, stress management, and resilience-building

(Cavioni et al., 2020, 2023a). Comprehensive programmes should incorporate self-care practices, stress reduction techniques (e.g., mindfulness-based interventions), and coping strategies that support teachers in handling challenges while sustaining their professional dedication. These programmes should also foster key competencies such as self-regulation, coping skills, help-seeking behaviours, and self-compassion.

Developing teachers' social and emotional competencies to improve classroom interactions. Teachers require explicit training in social and emotional skills that support positive classroom interactions and relationship-building with students. Research has demonstrated that teachers act as emotion socializers, influencing students' emotional development through their expressiveness, regulation, and knowledge of emotions (Denham et al., 2012). Teachers' ability to model appropriate emotional expression, provide supportive reactions to students' emotions, and facilitate emotion-focused discussions has been linked to students' improved emotional intelligence, self-regulation, and prosocial behaviours. Despite increasing recognition of teachers' role in fostering students' emotional well-being, research indicates that many educators receive little to no formal training in emotional literacy. Explicit professional development programmes focusing on teachers' social and emotional competence could help them become more aware of their own emotions, improve their reactions to students, and adopt more effective emotion-based teaching strategies. As schools continue to emphasize social and emotional learning as a key educational goal, investing in teachers' own emotional competence is essential to ensuring they can effectively model and support these skills in students.

Strengthening teachers' beliefs about mental health promotion. Another essential aspect of integrating mental health promotion in schools involves teachers' beliefs about their role in fostering students' well-being and social-emotional development (Brackett et al., 2012). Research suggests that educators who adopt a growth mindset—the belief that social-emotional skills, like academic abilities, can be developed over time—experience lower emotional exhaustion, greater emotional control, and more adaptive coping strategies (Nalipay et al., 2021). When teachers perceive emotions as malleable and actively engage in emotion regulation, they are more likely to reframe stressful situations, focus on positive aspects, and cultivate pleasant emotional experiences. Having a growth mindset towards mental health promotion is not only beneficial for teachers' well-being but also influences their willingness to embed mental health practices in their daily teaching routines. Educators who view students' mental health development as equally important as academic subjects are more committed to implementing social-emotional learning activities, thus reinforcing a whole-school culture of well-being. However, a critical challenge is that some teachers do not see mental health promotion as part of their professional responsibilities. This perception often stems from the blurred boundaries between education, healthcare, and social work, leading some teachers to feel that mental health interventions fall outside their role (Weston et al., 2018). Additionally, there is a risk of teachers perceiving school-based mental health programmes as an additional burden rather than an integral part of their teaching practice. Some educators may believe that supporting students' social-emotional development is primarily the responsibility of parents, while others may view mental health programmes as extraneous initiatives rather than fundamental components of education. To overcome these barriers, teachers must receive guidance and institutional support to integrate mental health promotion into their professional role. By reinforcing the educational value of mental health skills and their impact on student success, schools can foster a shared commitment to mental health promotion, leading to both improved teacher well-being and more effective student support.

Enhancing teachers' readiness and mental health literacy. Teachers' perceived readiness to implement mental health programmes plays a crucial role in the quality and effectiveness of programme delivery (Cavioni et al., 2023a). Readiness involves not only competence and self-efficacy in delivering mental health-related content but also the belief that such programmes enhance teaching effectiveness and student outcomes (Weston et al., 2018). Many teachers express a lack of preparedness in addressing mental health topics in the classroom. Research suggests that educators frequently experience a sense of inadequacy when implementing mental health programmes, especially in responding to students' emotional and psychological needs (Weston et al., 2018). In some cases, teachers may lack confidence in how to address mental health issues that arise during programme delivery, which can hinder effective implementation (Askell-Williams et al., 2007; Yamaguchi et al., 2021).

A key factor in teacher readiness is mental health literacy, which encompasses knowledge, strategies, and skills essential for identifying, preventing, and addressing mental health concerns in school settings (Jorm et al., 1997). Mental health literacy empowers teachers to create supportive learning environments, recognize early warning signs of mental health difficulties, and facilitate positive student relationships. However, without formal mental health training, teachers tend to focus more on externalizing behaviours (e.g., aggression, hyperactivity) while overlooking internalizing issues (e.g., anxiety, depression). Externalizing problems are generally more overt and disruptive, often involving verbal or physical aggression, defiance, or destruction of property. These behaviours demand immediate attention in the classroom, as they interfere with learning, disrupt the environment, and require direct intervention from teachers, compelling them to pause their instruction and manage the situation. In contrast, internalizing problems are less visible and more difficult to detect, as they manifest internally rather than through outward expressions of distress. Students experiencing anxiety, depression, or social withdrawal may appear quiet, compliant, or disengaged, making it less likely that their struggles will be immediately recognized. Although these students may not disrupt classroom activities, they remain at significant psychological risk, as their distress often goes unnoticed or is misinterpreted as a lack of participation or motivation (Patalay & Fitzsimons, 2018). This discrepancy in teachers' responses may be driven by implicit biases, leading them to underestimate the severity of internalizing problems while prioritizing the management of disruptive behaviours. Failing to address internalizing difficulties can result in long-term negative consequences, including academic decline, social isolation, and an increased risk of mental health disorders. To enhance teachers' readiness, schools should provide training and resources tailored to educators' needs, including practical guidelines, structured supervision, and accessible terminology to help teachers navigate mental health concepts. For instance, using "teacher-friendly" glossaries to define mental health difficulties and conducting guided supervision sessions can help educators develop the confidence to support students' social-emotional needs. Moreover, integrating mental health literacy into daily school practices enables teachers to connect mental health skills with academic instruction, apply active learning strategies, and foster strong teacher-student relationships.

Building on the key aspects discussed in the previous sections, the following section introduces two European projects—Promoting Mental Health at Schools (PROMEHS) and Teaching to Be (T2Be). These initiatives aim to integrate various dimensions of mental health promotion within school settings, offering comprehensive approaches to fostering well-being in education. Both projects were funded by the European Commission under Key Action 3 of Erasmus+, which supports policy reform in education and training. Unlike other Erasmus+ initiatives, these projects require collaboration with policymakers to ensure effective implementation and long-term sustainability. This approach bridges research-based innovations with large-scale policy adoption, integrating evidence-based mental health strategies into national education frameworks.

4.2 The PROMEHS Project

The PROMEHS programme represents a comprehensive initiative designed to address the escalating mental health needs within school communities, with a particular emphasis on teachers' well-being. Implemented in six European countries during the COVID-19 pandemic, a period marked by heightened psychological challenges globally, PROMEHS employed a systemic approach to mental health promotion. PROMEHS was conceptualized as a universal programme, meaning it is aimed to be implemented across entire school populations rather than targeting specific at-risk groups. It is also an evidence-based initiative, which was designed, implemented, and assessed by applying robust scientific research and collecting empirical data employing validated instruments to measure the expected outcomes. Its theoretical foundation integrates three central themes: the promotion of social and emotional learning, the promotion of resilience, and the prevention of social, emotional, and behavioural problems (Cavioni et al., 2020).

The implementation of PROMEHS was carried out in Italy, Greece, Romania, Portugal, Latvia, and Croatia during the 2020–2021 school year. It involved 687 teachers (94% female) across 434 classrooms in 124 schools, spanning all educational levels, from kindergarten to upper secondary. Schools were randomly assigned to one of two research conditions: 363 teachers participated in the experimental group, while 324 teachers were assigned to the waiting list control group. The effectiveness of PROMEHS was evaluated using a quasi-experimental research design (Cefai et al., 2022), which is a method that assesses intervention effects by comparing groups that are not randomly assigned. Teachers' outcomes were compared between an experimental group (which received the intervention) and a waiting list group (which received the programme later). The research followed three phases: pre-test, intervention, and post-test. The pre-test was conducted at the beginning of the 2020–2021 academic year to establish baseline measures. During the intervention phase, teachers in the experimental group implemented the PROMEHS programme over a period of six months, whereas those in the waiting list group did not take part in this phase. Finally, the post-test was administered at the end of the academic year to evaluate changes. Afterwards, the waiting list group also received the intervention.

The PROMEHS teacher training consisted of a total of 25 hours: 16 hours were delivered at the beginning of the school year, while the remaining 9 hours were provided as ongoing supervision throughout the programme's implementation. Initially, the training offered both theoretical knowledge and practical guidance on promoting mental health in schools. Teachers were trained to implement activities from the PROMEHS curriculum, which includes seven handbooks tailored to students, parents, and educators. Supervision included three group meetings, and they served a dual purpose. First, they aimed to collaboratively evaluate with teachers the progress of implementing the PROMEHS activities in the classroom. This involved evaluating whether teachers implemented the activities according to the initial guidelines and identifying any challenges or obstacles they faced, either in their own execution of the activities or in students' level of engagement. The second objective was to offer psychological support to teachers.

The PROMEHS programme was implemented during the COVID-19 pandemic, a period marked by significant difficulties in managing online teaching and maintaining meaningful relationships with students through virtual platforms (Conte et al., 2023). These challenges disrupted traditional forms of interaction, complicating teachers' ability to foster connections with students and effectively monitor their academic progress. To address these issues, the supervision sessions provided a group setting where teachers could openly share their emotional and social difficulties. This created a supportive space aimed at enhancing teachers' psychological well-being. By fostering an environment of mutual support and shared reflection, the sessions were instrumental in promoting teacher well-being and in ensuring the effective implementation of the PROMEHS programme. Table 4.1 provides an overview of the topics covered in the teacher training course and supervision sessions.

PROMEHS offers a comprehensive framework for children and adolescents aged 3–18, providing resources tailored for both classroom implementation and home-based activities involving parents. The programme's seven handbooks include four that focus on structured, age-appropriate activities for teachers and students, facilitating the seamless incorporation of mental health practices into daily educational routines. The remaining three handbooks serve as specialized resources for promoting mental health among teachers, parents, school leaders, and policy-makers, addressing the needs of all stakeholders within the school ecosystem (Cefai et al., 2022; Grazzani et al., 2022). One handbook is specifically dedicated to supporting teacher mental health. This resource provides both theoretical and practical knowledge on promoting social and emotional learning, building resilience, and addressing social, emotional, and behavioural difficulties in the school context. It outlines strategies for implementing individual and group interventions, equipping educators with tools to create a positive and supportive classroom environment while maintaining their own well-being. Another handbook targets parents, offering guidance on reinforcing mental health practices at home and effectively utilizing the programme's resources. Parents engage through tailored webinars, which offer practical advice on supporting their children's emotional and social development, fostering a cohesive approach to mental health across school and home settings. The

Table 4.1 Topics addressed in the training course and the supervision for teachers

Topics		
Teachers' mental health	Students' mental health	Contents of the PROMEHS curriculum
• *Enhancing own educators' well-being* by applying active listening techniques, fostering peer support by sharing experiences, and offering evidence-based strategies to mitigate stress, promote a harmonious work-life integration, and cultivate a strong and positive professional identity • *Providing teachers with SEL skills* to recognize their own emotions, strengths, and limitations to foster self-confidence; manage challenging emotions effectively; demonstrate empathy towards members of the school community; build meaningful relationships; communicate constructively and positively resolve conflicts; and make ethical, impactful decisions that benefit school staff, students, and their families • *Strengthening teachers' resilience* to effectively manage stress, frustration, and anxiety, while recognizing the importance of seeking support when needed. It includes also proactively and flexibly adapting to changes and challenges, maintaining a positive outlook in the face of adversity, and establishing healthy boundaries to prevent burnout and safeguard overall well-being	• *Observing and fostering students' social and emotional skills* to create a safe, supportive, and inclusive environment that promotes their psychological well-being. Identifying and implementing effective best practices within the curricular teaching framework to address these needs and ensure their integration into daily educational activities • Highlighting the pivotal role of *teachers as role models* which involves demonstrating healthy emotional regulation, empathy, and effective communication. Teachers' behaviours and emotional expressions significantly influence students' ability to recognize, understand, which are essential for fostering students' social and emotional development • Developing and implementing strategies to promote well-being applying and holistic approach that prioritizes the *collective well-being of the entire school community*. This perspective emphasizes fostering a *sense of belonging and connectedness* among all members—students, teachers, and staff	• Providing a detailed *description and explanation of the three core PROMEHS themes*, encompassing a thorough exploration of strategies to promote social and emotional learning, foster resilience, and prevent social, emotional, and behavioural difficulties in children and adolescents • Offering comprehensive guidance on the *use of project materials and the implementation of PROMEHS activities*, equipping teachers with practical tools to effectively incorporate these activities into classroom practices and home-based learning environments

third handbook is designed for school leaders and policymakers, emphasizing the importance of systemic integration and the sustainability of mental health initiatives.

In addition to these handbooks, teachers received specialized glossaries tailored to their educational level and the age group of their students. These glossaries included the most frequently used terms related to school-based mental health promotion, as introduced during training sessions and referenced in the PROMEHS manuals. Each term was clearly defined and accompanied by practical examples illustrating how it manifests in the classroom setting. The mental health glossaries served as essential tools for enhancing teachers' understanding and application of key psychological concepts in their professional practice. By providing a shared language for discussing mental health topics, these glossaries facilitated greater confidence in recognizing and addressing students' emotional and social needs. Additionally, they helped reduce stigma surrounding mental health issues by ensuring that educators had accurate and accessible terminology to integrate these discussions naturally into their teaching. The structured vocabulary also supported teachers' own mental health awareness, enabling them to reflect on their emotional well-being and adopt evidence-based strategies for stress management and resilience-building within the school environment.

PROMEHS activities are designed with objectives aimed at promoting specific skills tailored to the developmental stage and age of the students. Teachers are encouraged to choose activities based on two levels of complexity: basic or advanced. Each activity session can last between 1–2 h and employs a variety of methodologies, including story reading, games, physical activities, multimedia resources, and more. Every activity includes a brief description of its learning objectives, the recommended age group, the difficulty level, and the materials required. Additionally, each activity includes several key components. It begins with a short story featuring one or more PROMEHS protagonists, followed by a series of questions designed to facilitate comprehension and encourage group discussion. Practical activities are incorporated, utilizing various methodologies to engage students in active learning. To assess progress, an evaluation grid is provided to monitor students' learning outcomes. The activity concludes with a clear explanation of its objectives, ensuring that students understand its purpose. Furthermore, teachers receive suggestions on how to integrate the targeted skills into daily classroom lessons and activities, along with additional resources to extend and deepen learning.

The stories introduced at the beginning of each activity depicted life events involving one or more recurring main characters. These characters appeared consistently throughout the activities and were shown evolving across different school levels, from kindergarten to secondary school. This continuity enabled students to witness the protagonists' growth and development over time, fostering a sense of identification and connection while enhancing the coherence of their learning experience. The characters of the PROMEHS programme were also designed to reflect diverse cultural traditions. For instance, Luca, one of the characters, has a name that is common in Italy, while Borna is a frequently used name in Croatia. This approach ensures that the curriculum features children with names representing various cultural contexts. The stories intentionally feature protagonists with diverse physical characteristics and cultural backgrounds, such as children with varying skin tones, Asian features, or distinctive traits like freckles, glasses, or vitiligo. These specific attributes, which can sometimes be sources of embarrassment or self-consciousness for children who possess them, were deliberately included to further emphasize the value of diversity in all its forms, including physical appearance. Open-ended questions are also integrated into each activity to encourage dialogue with students. Teachers are prompted to stimulate reflection by asking questions such as "*What did you learn today*?" at the end of the session. After a certain period (e.g., the end of a term), teachers can also ask students to reflect on and describe their progress in the skills covered during the activities. The activities are integrated into the school curriculum, and to maximize their benefits, it is recommended that the skills developed through the PROMEHS activities be practised and reinforced beyond the weekly hours dedicated to the programme.

The activities were designed following the principles of the S.A.F.E. model (Durlak et al., 2011; Cipriano et al., 2023), to ensure structured learning and effective skill development. S.A.F.E. stands for "sequenced", "active", "focused", and "explicit", and each component plays a critical role in the design and implementation of the activities.

"Sequenced" refers to the systematic organization of activities, where each is carefully planned to build upon previously acquired skills. This cumulative approach allows learners to develop competencies progressively and effectively, reinforcing prior knowledge while introducing new concepts in a logical sequence. "Active" emphasizes the importance of experiential learning. The activities engage participants in hands-on methods, such as role-playing, interactive discussions, or practical exercises. These methods encourage active participation, making the learning process more meaningful and ensuring that the skills are practised in real-life contexts. "Focused" ensures that each activity is designed with clear and specific objectives. This targeted approach allows the intervention to concentrate on key competencies, avoiding dispersion and ensuring that the learning goals are met effectively. "Explicit" highlights the need for clarity in the delivery of the activities. Detailed instructions and clearly defined goals are provided to both educators and participants, ensuring that everyone understands the purpose and expected outcomes of the activities. This clarity supports consistent implementation and enhances the likelihood of achieving the desired skill development.

4.2.1 Evaluating the Impact of PROMEHS

The evaluation utilized self-report questionnaires to examine teachers' social and emotional competence, resilience, and self-efficacy. To assess social and emotional competence, the Social and Emotional Competence of Teachers (SECTRS; Grazzani et al., 2024; Tom, 2012) was administered. This instrument consists of 25 items evaluating four dimensions: teacher-student relationships (positive interactions between teachers and students), emotion regulation (teachers' capacity to manage emotions during challenging situations), social awareness (sensitivity to diversity and awareness of how teaching practices influence students), and interpersonal relationships (teachers' interactions with parents and school staff). Responses were recorded on a six-point Likert scale, ranging from 1 (strongly disagree) to 6 (strongly agree). In the original version of the instrument, Cronbach's alpha coefficients for the four subscales ranged from .69 to .81 (Tom, 2012). In the present study, reliability coefficients for the same subscales ranged from .72 to .82 at pre-test, and from .73 to .80 at post-test.

Teachers' resilience was measured using the Connor-Davidson Resilience Scale (CD-RISC 10; Connor & Davidson, 2003), a ten-item self-report questionnaire designed to evaluate the ability to cope with adversity. Items are rated on a five-point Likert scale, from 0 (not true at all) to 4 (true nearly all the time). Cronbach's alpha coefficients were .88 at the pre-test and .89 at post-test, aligning closely with the reliability reported for the original instrument ($\alpha = .85$).

Self-efficacy was assessed with the Ohio State Teacher Efficacy Scale (OSTES; Tschannen-Moran & Woolfolk Hoy, 2001). This instrument evaluates three key aspects of teachers' self-efficacy: Efficacy for Student Engagement, Efficacy for Instructional Strategies, and Efficacy for Classroom Management. The questionnaire comprises 12 items, each rated on a nine-point Likert scale, enabling detailed insight into teachers' perceived efficacy in these domains. Cronbach's alpha coefficients for the three subscales ranged from .81 to .86, consistent with the reliability estimates reported for the original instrument (Tschannen-Moran & Woolfolk Hoy, 2001).

To assess the equivalence of the two groups before the intervention, a series of analyses of variance were conducted to compare teachers' pre-test scores based on group assignments. Additionally, the effectiveness of the intervention on teachers' social and emotional learning, resilience, and self-efficacy was examined using repeated-measures analyses of variance, with time (pre-test Vs post-test) as the within-subject factor and group condition (experimental vs. waiting list control) as the between-subject factor. The dependent variables, measured at both time points, included teachers' scores on social and emotional learning, self-efficacy, and resilience.

A statistically significant improvement was observed in the experimental group across all the assessed variables. Specifically, teachers in the experimental group demonstrated substantial gains in their *social and emotional competence* compared to the waiting list group. Notably, teachers in the experimental group showed enhanced quality in the relationships they established and maintained with their students, despite the challenges posed by the pandemic, which limited face-to-face interactions. Additionally, their scores in emotion regulation increased from pre- to post-test. This is particularly relevant as teachers regularly face demanding situations, such as maintaining classroom discipline and managing a heavy workload, which requires the ability to connect with and effectively regulate their emotions. Teachers who participated in the PROMEHS programme demonstrated higher levels of social awareness, becoming more attentive and empathetic towards their students. This heightened awareness had a positive ripple effect on their professional engagement, as they were more deliberate in selecting and implementing teaching practices that prioritized students' needs and overall well-being. These adjustments significantly enhanced students' motivation and classroom dynamics. Moreover, the programme contributed to strengthening teachers' relationships not only with their students but also with other members of the school community. This underscored the intervention's broader impact in fostering a more cohesive and supportive educational environment.

The PROMEHS programme demonstrated a significant positive impact on teachers' *resilience*, as evidenced by higher resilience scores reported by the experimental group at the post-test compared to the waiting list group. This improvement can be attributed to the programme's carefully designed methodology and the content provided during the training sessions and supervision meetings. Teachers were equipped with specific training to enhance their understanding of coping mechanisms and strategies to manage stress and adversity effectively. Given the programme's emphasis on self-awareness, participants were further empowered to identify their psychological needs, allowing them to take proactive steps towards prioritizing their mental health. Supervision and monitoring contributed to the programme's success by fostering a sense of confidence and competence among teachers in delivering the curriculum content. Regular feedback and guidance during these sessions helped teachers feel supported and prepared, reducing feelings of isolation and uncertainty in their professional roles. Beyond individual benefits, the programme also encouraged the development of collective psychological resources within the school environment. By promoting trust and collaboration among colleagues, the intervention created a supportive network that enabled teachers to address challenges together. This collective resilience not only strengthened their ability to manage adversity but also contributed to a more cohesive and effective educational community.

PROMEHS also demonstrated significant effectiveness in enhancing teachers' *self-efficacy*. Teachers who participated in the programme's training and implementation reported feeling more confident in their ability to engage and motivate students, manage classroom dynamics effectively, and employ instructional strategies to teach subject content competently. Furthermore, data analysis revealed that an increase in the number of activities implemented in the classroom was associated with improved teacher well-being.

During supervision sessions, teachers shared that their increased self-efficacy translated into greater confidence in their professional capacities. This boost in confidence was closely linked to higher job satisfaction, motivation, and enthusiasm for teaching. Enhanced self-efficacy also contributed to the delivery of higher-quality instruction. Teachers who believe in their ability to achieve desired outcomes are more likely to approach teaching with a proactive and problem-solving mindset, tailoring their instructional strategies to better meet the diverse needs of their students (Cavioni, Toto, & Ornaghi, 2023b). This, in turn, created a more engaging and effective learning environment, where students were more likely to thrive academically and socially. Moreover, teachers reported experiencing reduced levels of stress. This can be attributed to the programme's focus on equipping them with practical tools and strategies to manage the challenges of teaching more effectively. Teachers with higher self-efficacy are better able to cope with demanding situations, such as managing disruptive behaviours or balancing competing professional responsibilities, as they perceive these challenges as manageable rather than overwhelming. This reduced stress not only benefited their mental health but also positively impacted their teaching performance, creating a more positive classroom atmosphere for both teachers and students. Overall, the programme fostered a cycle where improved self-efficacy, reduced stress, and enhanced instructional quality reinforced one another, contributing to sustainable improvements in teachers' professional and personal well-being.

4.3 The Teaching to Be Project

This section presents the European project entitled "Teaching to Be (T2Be): supporting teachers' professional growth and well-being in the field of social and emotional learning", which introduced an innovative approach to teacher training by integrating gamification principles instead of relying on traditional in-person or online courses. The project aimed to improve teachers' well-being using serious games, providing an engaging and interactive learning experience. Conducted between 2021 and 2024, it involved researchers, schools, policymakers, and various stakeholders from Austria, Latvia, Lithuania, Norway, Italy, Slovenia, Spain, and Portugal.

Gamification refers to the application of game design elements and principles in non-game contexts to enhance motivation, engagement, and learning outcomes (Deterding, 2012). It involves integrating elements such as challenges, rewards, storytelling, and feedback mechanisms to create an immersive and dynamic learning environment (Sailer et al., 2017). In educational contexts, serious games have primarily been developed for student engagement, focusing on enhancing learning outcomes across various academic subjects and fostering skills related to well-being and health education (Cichy et al., 2020; Chen et al., 2023). However, the creation of serious games specifically targeting teachers' professional development remains relatively limited. For example, the "Kiddo" game was designed to facilitate teacher-led discussions on gender equality, providing school-aged children with opportunities to explore gender stereotypes through interactive, decision-making scenarios (Yañez et al., 2023). Similarly, the SRL-4Ts game, inspired by the Trivial Pursuit board game, aims to support teachers in developing collaborative activities that promote students' self-regulated learning skills (Persico et al., 2023). While these initiatives involve teachers, their primary focus is on enhancing student competencies rather than directly addressing the professional growth or personal development of educators. To date, there is limited evidence of serious games being employed specifically to support teachers' professional well-being. To address this gap, the T2be project was developed to offer teachers a structured, yet adaptable and engaging framework that leverages gamification to enhance their social and emotional competencies, strengthen their stress management skills, and promote overall well-being. The following sections will outline the stages involved in the development of the content for the programme named "Online Wellbeing Course (OWC)", its key features, and its success in promoting teachers' well-being.

4.3.1 The Online Wellbeing Course

The development of the OWG followed a two-phase process. Initially, a comprehensive literature review was conducted to identify risk and protective factors influencing teachers' well-being. This analysis focused on work-related stress, burnout, and emotional exhaustion, as well as protective factors such as social and emotional learning competencies, including self-awareness, self-management, social awareness, relationship skills, and responsible decision-making. The review provided a strong foundation for designing the game to support teachers' well-being. In the second phase, a Participatory Action Research (PAR) approach was used to refine the game's content based on teachers' real-world experiences. PAR actively involves participants, fostering co-creation where teachers contribute insights, provide feedback, and shape the intervention. This enhances the game's relevance and effectiveness while empowering educators by valuing their expertise (Baum et al., 2006). A sample of 86 in-service teachers participated in focus groups, providing feedback and suggestions through structured discussions guided by open-ended questions. This collaborative process ensured that the game was both practical and aligned with teachers' needs. To capture insights comprehensively, discussions were documented through audio recordings and written notes, with participant consent. Summaries were shared with teachers for validation, facilitating further refinements.

The game consisted of 12 levels, structured to be completed over five months, with each level targeting specific well-being related objectives (see Table 4.2). To create an immersive and engaging experience, the game incorporated various features that encouraged self-reflection and active participation, effectively capturing and maintaining teachers'

Table 4.2 Overview of the OWC levels

Level	Aims
1	This level introduces the programme, providing participants with a foundational understanding of its purpose and structure. It emphasizes the *importance of well-being in the educational context* and its impact on personal and professional life. Teachers are encouraged to reflect on their professional well-being, identifying *factors that influence their health and job satisfaction*. The level also guides educators in distinguishing between *challenges* they can control and those beyond their influence, fostering problem-solving skills, adaptive coping strategies, and resilience in their professional roles
2	This level aims to help teachers *recognize their strengths* and effectively integrate them into their professional practice. It introduces the S.M.A.R.T. methodology, a structured approach to setting and achieving goals. This method ensures that objectives are specific, measurable, achievable, relevant, and time-bound, providing a clear framework for effective goal-setting
	Teachers are guided in identifying both personal and professional objectives while developing strategies to track their progress. By following this structured approach, they gain greater clarity in defining their goals, establish realistic milestones, and enhance their ability to stay committed to their objectives. Through this process, participants strengthen their self-efficacy and goal-directed behaviour, fostering a proactive mindset towards both personal and professional growth
3	This level focuses on exploring the *connection between emotions, behaviours, and beliefs*, emphasizing their influence on teachers' professional and personal experiences. Participants are encouraged to critically examine factors that may interfere with or hinder the development of meaningful and high-quality social relationships within the school environment
4	This level aims to help teachers identify *sources of social support* across different life contexts and apply strategies to foster positive relationships within the school environment. Participants are encouraged to strengthen their support networks and enhance collaboration, contributing to a more supportive and inclusive school climate
5	This level is designed to assist teachers in recognizing ineffective *time management habits* and adopting more effective strategies. Participants are encouraged to implement practical techniques to improve productivity and achieve a healthier balance between their professional and personal responsibilities

(continued)

Table 4.2 (continued)

Level	Aims
6	This level is intended to encourage teachers to reflect on the significance of *effective classroom management strategies* and their impact on the learning environment. Participants will explore and identify evidence-based strategies that enhance classroom dynamics and foster a positive atmosphere. Additionally, they will be guided in implementing these strategies in their daily practice to improve student engagement and overall classroom effectiveness
7	This level is designed to help teachers *recognize their stress responses* and accurately *identify their emotions*. Participants explore effective stress management strategies to enhance their emotional well-being and resilience in professional settings
8	This level aims to equip teachers with strategies to effectively *manage stressful* situations by enhancing their emotional responses and developing greater self-awareness. Participants learn techniques to recognize and regulate their emotional reactions and connect with their bodily sensations, fostering a holistic approach to stress management and overall well-being
9	This level is designed to promote *self-empathy*, which involves the ability to understand and accept one's own emotions and experiences with kindness and without self-judgment. Participants work on enhancing their capacity for *compassion* and *empathy* towards others by recognizing and respecting different perspectives. Additionally, they engage in self-reflection to appreciate their *intrinsic value*
10	This level aims to enhance teachers' *communication skills*, enabling them to express themselves effectively and engage in meaningful interactions within the educational environment. It encourages participants to critically analyse, evaluate, and reflect on their professional experiences and overall well-being
11	This level focuses on strengthening teachers' *self-confidence* and enhancing their *leadership skills*. It encourages participants to recognize their abilities, take initiative, and effectively influence their professional environment. Teachers develop the confidence needed to lead and inspire both students and colleagues to contribute to a more positive and dynamic school atmosphere
12	This level encourages teachers to reflect on their *work performance* to achieve better outcomes and enhance *productivity*. It promotes critical analysis of challenging situations, fostering the *ability to identify alternative and constructive solutions*. Through this reflective process, teachers develop problem-solving skills and a proactive approach to overcoming professional obstacles

attention throughout the gameplay. Although designed for individual use, teachers were also encouraged to discuss and share their reflections and acquired knowledge with colleagues in offline school settings.

A key component of the game was its narrative-driven structure, where each player assumed the role of a teacher avatar, fostering emotional engagement and connections to real-life experiences in the educational context. The storytelling element encouraged teachers to reflect on their experiences and empathize with their own and others' challenges. The game introduced participants to its storyline with a brief introductory video that established the context and goals. Subsequently, players received step-by-step guidance on navigating various scenarios and utilizing available tools to accomplish designated objectives. To further enhance the experience, immersive and interactive scenarios were incorporated, enabling teachers to engage with realistic and profession-specific challenges. These scenarios allowed teachers to explore different school environments, tackle diverse situations, and apply problem-solving strategies relevant to their role. By progressing through various challenges and levels, teachers could actively test their skills, adapt their responses, and gain practical insights into managing complex classroom dynamics and fostering a supportive learning environment. These scenarios provided opportunities for self-reflection, practising coping strategies, considering diverse perspectives in addressing social challenges, and assessing the potential consequences of their decisions within the school environment. The game also featured interactive elements, enabling teachers to engage with virtual characters and objects within the environment to enhance their learning experience. These interactions, such as communicating with virtual colleagues or students, helped teachers practice effective communication and empathy (see Fig. 4.1).

Another significant aspect of the game was the inclusion of an inventory system that allowed teachers to collect and utilize various items throughout their gameplay. This feature encouraged problem-solving skills and creative thinking, as teachers could strategically use collected objects to overcome challenges and progress through the game. Reflection prompts were also embedded throughout the gameplay at critical decision points, encouraging teachers to pause and reflect on their experiences, emotions, and thoughts regarding different aspects of school life.

Fig. 4.1 Example of interaction between the main character and other teachers within the school

These prompts, often presented as short quizzes (see Fig. 4.2), facilitated deeper insights into their personal well-being and professional challenges.

To support continuous development, the game incorporated a comprehensive feedback and progress monitoring system. This feature provided visual indicators of progress, such as earned points and performance summaries, enabling teachers to track their growth in key social and emotional competencies. The feedback mechanism fostered self-awareness by highlighting strengths, areas for improvement, and the broader impact of their actions on themselves and others. This system provided immediate reinforcement for teachers' efforts, fostering a sense of accomplishment, progression, and measurable success. Real-time performance evaluations allowed teachers to identify mistakes and make immediate adjustments, while the gamification elements made the learning process more engaging and enjoyable (Faiella & Ricciardi, 2015). Additionally, the game featured integrated short videos designed to enrich the learning experience by providing in-depth knowledge on key well-being topics. These videos covered a broad spectrum of subjects, including stress management techniques, self-care strategies, effective communication, and fostering positive relationships. The combination of visual and auditory learning facilitated better retention and comprehension of critical concepts, offering teachers an immersive and interactive learning experience tailored to their professional needs.

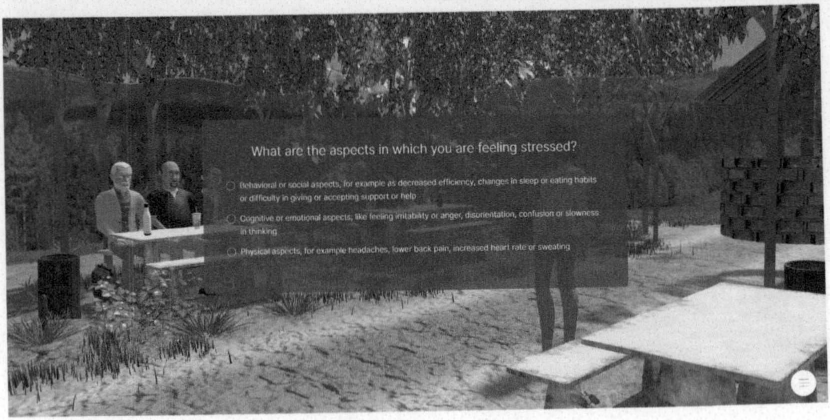

Fig. 4.2 Example of self-reflection-oriented questions

An additional resource provided to support the learning experience was a digital handbook (Talič et al., 2023), designed to complement the serious game and promote self-reflection among participating teachers. The handbook was distributed alongside game access and served as a structured guide to facilitate reflection and the practical application of concepts and skills acquired throughout the gameplay. It was specifically designed to align with the different levels and objectives of the game, ensuring coherence and continuity in learning. The handbook featured a variety of activities aimed at fostering deeper engagement and self-awareness. These activities included self-assessment tools, goal-setting exercises, open-ended reflection prompts, and journaling opportunities to encourage teachers to explore their experiences in a more introspective manner. By complementing the interactive aspects of the serious game with reflective tasks, the handbook supported a comprehensive understanding of key concepts and encouraged participants to share their insights with colleagues in offline settings reinforcing collaborative learning and professional development. Figure 4.3 presents two examples of activities included in the handbook that accompanies the OWC.

The study sample consisted of 189 Italian teachers from 10 Italian schools. Participants were granted access to the OWC for five months, from late November 2022 to early April 2023. Each teacher was provided with an individual user account, allowing them to access the game through Gamelearn (www.game-learn.com), an online learning platform

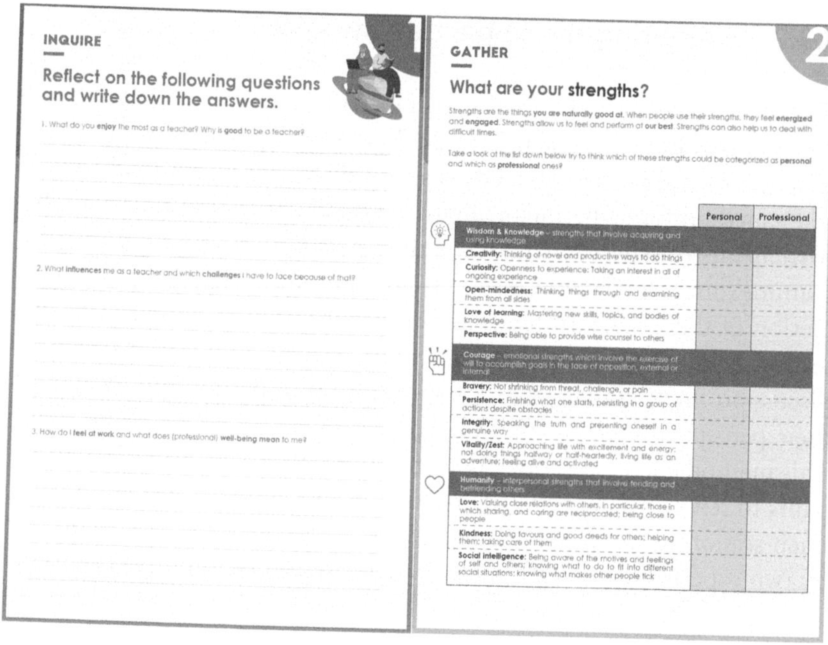

INQUIRE

Reflect on the following questions and write down the answers.

1. What do you **enjoy** the most as a teacher? Why is **good** to be a teacher?

2. What **influences** me as a teacher and which **challenges** I have to face because of that?

3. How do I **feel at work** and what does (professional) **well-being mean** to me?

2

GATHER

What are your **strengths?**

Strengths are the things **you are naturally good at**. When people use their strengths, they feel **energized** and **engaged**. Strengths allow us to feel and perform at **our best**. Strengths can also help us to deal with difficult times.

Take a look at the list down below try to think which of these strengths could be categorized as **personal** and which as **professional** ones?

	Personal	Professional
Wisdom & Knowledge – strengths that involve acquiring and using knowledge		
Creativity: Thinking of novel and productive ways to do things		
Curiosity: Openness to experience: Taking an interest in all of ongoing experience		
Open-mindedness: Thinking things through and examining them from all sides		
Love of learning: Mastering new skills, topics, and bodies of knowledge		
Perspective: Being able to provide wise counsel to others		
Courage – emotional strengths which involve the exercise of will to accomplish goals in the face of opposition, external or internal		
Bravery: Not shrinking from threat, challenge, or pain		
Persistence: Finishing what one starts, persisting in a group of actions despite obstacles		
Integrity: Speaking the truth and presenting oneself in a genuine way		
Vitality/Zest: Approaching life with excitement and energy; not doing things halfway or half-heartedly, living life as an adventure; feeling alive and activated		
Humanity – interpersonal strengths that involve tending and befriending others		
Love: Valuing close relations with others, in particular, those in which sharing, and caring are reciprocated; being close to people		
Kindness: Doing favours and good deeds for others; helping them; taking care of them		
Social intelligence: Being aware of the motives and feelings of self and others; knowing what to do to fit into different social situations; knowing what makes other people tick		

Fig. 4.3 Sample activities from the handbook provided as a complementary resource to the OWC (Talič et al., 2023)

designed to enable flexible engagement at their convenience. To ensure a structured and balanced learning experience, participants were required to complete one level per week, accommodating their professional responsibilities while maintaining consistent engagement. To promote participant retention and sustained involvement, several strategies were implemented. The game was structured with clear weekly objectives and milestones, offering a sense of progress and accomplishment that encouraged continued participation. Additionally, regular communication was maintained throughout the study, with updates, reminders, and motivational messages delivered via an anonymous internal messaging system embedded within the platform. These notifications served to keep participants informed, encourage, and reinforce the importance of their ongoing engagement in the programme. Collectively, these approaches fostered motivation and created a supportive environment conducive to active participation in the study.

4.3.2 Evaluating the Impact of the OWC

A qualitative research design was employed to evaluate the effectiveness of the programme, allowing for an in-depth exploration of teachers' experiences and perceptions. Focus group discussions were conducted as a key method for gathering qualitative insights, providing a platform for participants to reflect on and share their perspectives regarding the programme's impact (Cavioni et al., 2024). Specifically, following the completion of the OWC, 10 focus group sessions were organized, with one session held in each participating school. A focus group is a structured discussion method that gathers a small group of participants to explore their perceptions, attitudes, and experiences regarding a specific topic. This method encourages open dialogue and interaction, allowing participants to reflect on their shared experiences in a supportive environment. Each session involved approximately 18–20 teachers and was facilitated by two experts experienced in qualitative research techniques. The facilitators provided a brief overview of the session's objectives, created a safe and respectful space for discussion, and encouraged active participation. The discussions lasted between 45 to 60 minutes and were audio-recorded with participants' consent to ensure accurate data collection.

Thematic analysis, a qualitative method for identifying, analysing, and reporting patterns within data (Braun & Clarke, 2006), was used to examine the focus group discussions with teachers. The audio recordings were transcribed verbatim to ensure accuracy. Two independent researchers conducted the initial coding, identifying meaningful data units such as phrases and sentences. These codes were grouped into themes and sub-themes based on recurring patterns. An iterative process of comparison and refinement was carried out to ensure the themes accurately reflected participants' experiences. To enhance reliability and validity, a third researcher reviewed the final themes and sub-themes. Interrater agreement among the researchers was high, with a Cohen's kappa coefficient of $k = 0.91$.

Table 4.3 presents the themes identified through the thematic analysis along with their corresponding subthemes, providing a detailed description of their characteristics. Firstly, the intervention significantly enhanced teachers' emotional competence, helping them better recognize and regulate their emotions, cope with stress, and prevent burnout. This, in turn,

Table 4.3 Theme and sub-themes identified applied thematic analysis (adapted from Cavioni et al., 2024)

Themes	Subthemes	Illustrative statements
1. **Emotional competence** A prominent theme that emerged from the analysis was the participants' reported enhancement of their emotional competence	*Self-awareness*. Teachers indicated that the course facilitated a better understanding and recognition of their own emotions, as well as those of their colleagues and students. Engaging with the serious game enabled them to navigate various challenging scenarios, fostering a deeper comprehension of emotions and their influence on teaching and learning	"The game made me more attuned to my own feelings and reactions. I learned to think about how I feel, to be able to better recognize negative emotions and maintain a positive mindset"
	Emotional regulation. Participants reported an increased awareness of their emotional triggers, which empowered them to manage their responses more effectively both within and outside the classroom. The game's activities and reflective exercises provided valuable insights into their emotional processes and introduced strategies to regulate emotions constructively. This improved capacity contributed to a stronger sense of self-efficacy and self-esteem in their professional roles	"I often struggled with managing my emotions in the face of daily challenging situations. However, through the various suggestions, including reflective discussions with my colleagues, I have developed a greater ability to regulate and understand my emotions"

(*continued*)

Table 4.3 (continued)

Themes	Subthemes	Illustrative statements
	Stress and burnout management. Teachers acknowledged that the OWC introduced them to a variety of coping strategies and stress reduction techniques, such as mindfulness exercises and deep breathing. They became more attuned to their emotional, behavioural, and physical well-being, enabling them to take proactive measures to prevent severe stress and burnout. The game also offered a sense of playfulness and relaxation, serving as a temporary escape from professional stressors. This experience allowed participants to recharge and approach their work with renewed clarity and enthusiasm	"I gained a deeper awareness of how negative emotional states can influence my behaviours. This allowed me to recognize and acknowledge my emotions enabling me to respond more effectively to stressful situations and developing a greater sense of calmness"
2. **Self-caring strategies** A key theme that emerged from the analysis was the enhancement of self-care practices among participants, aimed at fostering their overall well-being. The serious game intervention served as a catalyst for self-reflection and personal growth, empowering teachers to effectively incorporate self-care into their daily routines	*Self-compassion*. Participants reported an increased ability to treat themselves with kindness, understanding, and acceptance, especially in challenging situations. Engaging with the serious game enabled teachers to cultivate a more compassionate attitude towards themselves, challenging self-critical and judgmental thoughts. The game's activities and narratives encouraged participants to reframe negative self-talk and adopt a more supportive internal dialogue. This shift in perspective allowed teachers to approach personal and professional challenges with greater empathy and self-acceptance, contributing to improved self-esteem and overall well-being	"Before the OWC, I often found myself being overly self-critical and judgmental, constantly striving for perfection and feeling inadequate. Now I try to be less critical of myself, to allow myself to make mistakes and not feel guilty"

(continued)

Table 4.3 (continued)

Themes	Subthemes	Illustrative statements
	Attention to one's own mental health. Teachers highlighted a heightened awareness of their mental well-being and an increased commitment to prioritizing self-care. The serious game, along with its accompanying handbook, provided structured opportunities for self-reflection, enabling participants to assess their well-being and adopt effective self-care strategies. Teachers acknowledged that the course equipped them with valuable tools to achieve a better work-life balance set personal boundaries, and manage time effectively, leading to more sustainable self-care habits. Additionally, the OWC fostered a sense of community among teachers, encouraging peer support and the exchange of self-care tips and experiences. Participants reported that the game helped normalize discussions around mental health and self-care within their schools, promoting a culture that values holistic well-being for both educators and students. This proactive approach to mental health awareness empowered teachers to take preventive actions and create a more supportive and mentally healthy educational environment	"Engaging with the game has been instrumental in helping me prioritize and pay attention to my own mental health. Prior, I often neglected my well-being, putting the needs of my students and overall school demands above my own. Now I feel I have learned the importance of self-care. The game served as a wake-up call, reminding me of the necessity to nurture my own wellbeing"

(continued)

Table 4.3 (continued)

Themes	Subthemes	Illustrative statements
3. Social awareness Teachers reported a significant improvement in their ability to demonstrate empathy, appreciation, and caring behaviours towards others. The serious game experience encouraged greater awareness of social dynamics within their professional environment	*Empathy towards others.* Participants indicated that the game encouraged them to reflect on their own biases and assumptions, which in turn enhanced their capacity to empathize with others. By engaging with the game's diverse characters and storylines, teachers were exposed to a variety of emotional experiences, fostering a deeper understanding of their colleagues' and students' emotions. This exposure contributed to greater emotional sensitivity and responsiveness in their professional interactions	"I have noticed that I have developed more attention toward the feelings of my colleagues. I tried to better observe their behaviours to understand how they felt to be more empathetic"
	Valuing the strengths of others. Teachers reported gaining valuable insights into the diverse experiences and perspectives of their colleagues and students, leading to an increased appreciation for their unique strengths and needs. This heightened awareness allowed teachers to tailor their support more effectively and foster a more inclusive and strengths-based approach in their interactions	"Participating in the game has had a profound impact on how I perceive and value others' abilities. Prior, I often focused on my own strengths and accomplishments. I discovered that some of my colleagues had skills that I didn't know, and I learned to value them more"

(continued)

Table 4.3 (continued)

Themes	Subthemes	Illustrative statements
	Caring for others. The serious game provided opportunities for teachers to practice navigating complex social interactions and develop strategies for fostering open, safe spaces for students to express their thoughts and emotions. As a result, participants felt more confident in facilitating discussions on students' emotional and social challenges, contributing to a more supportive and inclusive school climate where care and emotional well-being are prioritized	"I have developed a deeper attention to the emotional state of my colleagues and a more intentional attitude to care for others. I realized I am now more prone to understand the diverse needs and perspectives of those around me. I am more mindful of the impact of my words, gestures, and choices on others"
4. **Relationship skills** The Online Wellbeing Course (OWC) had a positive impact on teachers' relationship skills, enhancing their ability to communicate effectively, establish collaborative relationships, seek and provide support, and apply leadership strategies in their professional practice	*Communication*. Teachers reported improvements in their communication skills with colleagues, students, and families. The OWC simulated real-life dialogues and communication challenges, providing practical strategies for expressing thoughts, active listening, and conflict resolution. As a result, participants felt more confident in delivering constructive feedback to students and engaging in meaningful, collaborative discussions with peers	"The game encouraged me to practice active listening and choose my words carefully [...] allowing me to connect better with my peers and students and create a more open and non-judgmental dialogue"

(*continued*)

Table 4.3 (continued)

Themes	Subthemes	Illustrative statements
	Collaboration. Participants emphasized the value of peer support and collaborative learning experienced within the serious game and the accompanying handbook activities. They reported an increased recognition of the importance of collegial support in their professional development and well-being. The OWC provided opportunities to connect with peers, share experiences, and seek and offer advice, fostering a culture of mutual support. Engaging in these shared reflections helped teachers feel more comfortable reaching out to colleagues and contributing their knowledge in offline school settings. This enhanced collaboration not only reduced feelings of professional isolation but also positively influenced student engagement, motivation, and academic performance	"The game created a community of teachers where we could exchange ideas and support one another. I realized that we are all striving toward a common goal of creating a nurturing and enriching learning environment for our students"
	Leadership. Teachers highlighted an improved understanding of leadership principles and a greater capacity to apply them in their daily teaching practices. The game's motivational aspects, such as goal-setting, feedback, and recognition of strengths, provided teachers with strategies to inspire and engage students. As a result, participants felt more empowered to take on leadership roles within their classrooms and school communities, contributing to overall school improvement and fostering a positive learning environment	"I often doubted my abilities and hesitated to take on leadership roles. […]. I now feel empowered to share my ideas, take initiative, and advocate for positive change within my school community"

(*continued*)

Table 4.3 (continued)

Themes	Subthemes	Illustrative statements
5. **Decision-making** Engagement with the OWC enhanced teachers' critical thinking, problem-solving abilities, and overall decision-making skills, equipping them with tools to make more informed and reflective choices	*Critical thinking*. The interactive nature of the game allowed teachers to practice decision-making in a risk-free environment. Participants reported that the serious game provided opportunities to explore different perspectives, evaluate the consequences of their choices, and reflect on the outcomes. This process boosted their confidence and competence in making informed decisions in real-life teaching situations. The game incorporated evidence-based psychological strategies, prompting teachers to assess their teaching methods, consider alternative approaches, and identify areas for professional growth	"The game encouraged me to question my assumptions and beliefs [...]. It pushed me to better analyze information and look for alternative solutions to reach greater outcomes for me, my peers, and students"
	Evaluating the consequences of actions. Through reflection and evaluation, teachers developed a more thoughtful and deliberate approach to their professional practice, considering both short-term and long-term impacts of their actions on students' academic, social, and emotional development. Participants reported an increased awareness of how their professional decisions influence their students, colleagues, and the overall school environment. The OWC helped them cultivate a greater sense of responsibility and mindfulness in their teaching approach	"The game helped me to think critically and consider the potential impact of my decisions. This improved my ability to make effective and responsible ethical choices in my teaching practice"

(*continued*)

Table 4.3 (continued)

Themes	Subthemes	Illustrative statements
6. **School Climate** Participants reported a heightened commitment to fostering a positive school environment and acknowledged their influential role in shaping the atmosphere within their institutions	*Cohesion*. Teachers highlighted that their participation in the OWC contributed to a stronger sense of unity among staff members, enhancing overall school cohesion. The shared experience of engaging with the course established a common language and understanding, fostering deeper connections and collaboration among teachers. This strengthened sense of cohesion extended beyond the teaching staff, positively influencing interactions with students, parents, and the broader school community	"Sharing our experiences and hearing the stories of others, [...] helped me develop a deep sense of connection toward my peers"
	School belonging. Participants noted that the OWC positively influenced their sense of belonging within the school environment. Teachers reported that their enhanced well-being contributed to improved relationships with colleagues and administrative staff, leading to a stronger connection to their professional community. As a result, the course fostered a more inclusive and supportive school atmosphere, reinforcing teachers' commitment to their roles and the overall mission of their institutions	"I often felt isolated and disconnected within the school community, overwhelmed by the demands of my profession. [...] I began to realize that I am not alone in facing challenges and that we are all on this journey together. I no longer feel isolated but rather an integral part of our school community"

fostered a more inclusive and supportive learning environment, improving their responsiveness to students' emotional needs. Secondly, the OWC promoted self-care practices, encouraging teachers to adopt strategies such as mindfulness and relaxation techniques to prioritize their well-being. This focus on self-care contributed to improved resilience, reduced burnout, and more effective classroom management, ultimately enhancing their professional performance and engagement with students.

Teachers also reported improvements in social awareness, including increased empathy, appreciation for others, and caring behaviours. Engaging with the serious game's scenarios allowed teachers to better understand the emotions and experiences of students and colleagues, fostering stronger relationships and a more trusting school environment. Additionally, the OWC positively impacted teachers' collaboration and leadership skills, boosting their confidence in teamwork, communication, and problem-solving. Participants reported a greater willingness to take on responsibilities and actively engage in professional dialogues, which contributed to a more supportive work culture and improved instructional practices. Moreover, the intervention enhanced teachers' decision-making abilities, equipping them with critical thinking and reflective practices. The game provided a safe environment to practice decision-making, helping teachers make informed and ethical choices that benefit students and their learning experiences. Finally, these positive changes extended to the overall school climate, fostering a greater sense of cohesion and belonging among staff. A supportive and inclusive school environment contributed to higher job satisfaction, reduced stress, and enhanced professional fulfilment, ultimately benefiting both teachers and students..

4.4 Scaling Up Mental Health Interventions: Lessons from European Programmes

The findings presented in this chapter highlight the urgent need for systemic, school-based interventions to enhance teachers' mental health. Addressing teacher well-being is not an ancillary concern but a fundamental component of a sustainable and effective education system (OECD, 2024). Without explicit recognition of teacher mental health as a policy priority, interventions risk remaining fragmented and ineffective in addressing the structural factors contributing to stress, burnout, and professional disengagement. Research underscores the effectiveness of structured, evidence-based programmes such as PROMEHS and T2Be, which equip educators with the necessary tools to foster psychological resilience, emotional regulation, and stress management skills (Cefai et al., 2022; Cavioni et al., 2023a). These initiatives integrate mental health literacy, professional development, and emotional well-being strategies, ensuring that teachers receive ongoing support rather than temporary interventions. Unlike many initiatives that focus exclusively on students, these programmes recognize that a mentally healthy school environment cannot exist without psychologically well-supported teachers. By adopting a whole-school approach, involving teachers, students, parents, school leaders, and policymakers, they ensure that mental health promotion is embedded into the broader educational ecosystem.

Beyond their national relevance, PROMEHS and T2Be offer valuable insights at the European and international levels, demonstrating their adaptability and effectiveness across different cultural and educational systems. By providing free, research-informed intervention models, these programmes contribute to reducing inequalities in access to teacher mental health support, ensuring that educators across various socio-economic and institutional settings benefit from high-quality training (Weare & Nind, 2011). The involvement of policymakers further reinforces the importance of embedding teacher mental health initiatives within national educational frameworks, preventing these efforts from being fragmented or supplementary. The PROMEHS programme, through structured training sessions, continuous supervision, and practical resources, has demonstrated its effectiveness in enhancing teachers' social and emotional competence, resilience, and self-efficacy. Similarly, the T2Be programme has leveraged gamification to offer an engaging and interactive approach to professional development, fostering teachers' emotional awareness, stress management skills, and confidence in navigating classroom challenges. Given the increasing prevalence of mental health challenges among educators, particularly following the COVID-19 pandemic, large-scale, evidence-based interventions such as PROMEHS and T2Be provide a replicable model for strengthening teacher well-being on an international scale.

Promoting teacher mental health requires a fundamental cultural and institutional shift, challenging the persistent stigma surrounding psychological well-being in the profession. A crucial first step is ensuring that teacher well-being is explicitly recognized within school mental health policies. Without this acknowledgment, efforts to improve working conditions and emotional resilience will remain disjointed and ineffective. To ensure long-term impact, teacher mental health should not be viewed in isolation but as an integral part of educational policy and school-wide well-being frameworks. Schools and policymakers must actively promote open discussions on mental health within teacher education programmes, helping dismantle misconceptions and normalize help-seeking behaviours. Shifting the narrative from individual responsibility to shared institutional accountability is crucial in fostering a proactive approach to well-being among educators.

A paradigm shift is imperative—one that reframes school well-being as a dynamic and interconnected system in which teacher mental health is given the same priority as student well-being. Without such a commitment, the broader goal of fostering a thriving and sustainable education system will remain incomplete. Investing in teacher mental health is not a luxury but a fundamental requirement for long-term educational success. Future research should further explore the long-term impact of these interventions and identify scalable strategies to expand their reach, ensuring that teacher well-being remains a policy priority in educational systems worldwide.

References

Askell-Williams, H., Lawson, M. J., & Murray-Harvey, R. (2007). Teaching and learning about mental illness: An Australian perspective. *International Journal of Mental Health Promotion, 9*(4), 26–36. https://doi.org/10.1080/14623730.2007.9721846

Baum, F., MacDougall, C., & Smith, D. (2006). Participatory action research. *Journal of Epidemiology and Community Health, 60*(10), 854–857. https://doi.org/10.1136/jech.2004.028662

Brackett, M. A., Reyes, M. R., Rivers, S. E., Elbertson, N. A., & Salovey, P. (2012). Assessing teachers' beliefs about social and emotional learning. *Journal of Psychoeducational Assessment, 30*(3), 219–236. https://doi.org/10.1177/0734282911424879

Braun, V., & Clarke, V. (2006). Using thematic analysis in psychology. *Qualitative Research in Psychology, 3*(2), 77–101. https://doi.org/10.1191/1478088706qp063o

Cavioni, V., & Grazzani, I. (2023). *L'apprendimento sociale ed emotivo: Teorie e buone pratiche per promuovere la salute mentale a scuola [Social and emotional learning: Theories and best practices for promoting mental health at school]*. Il Mulino.

Cavioni, V., Grazzani, I., & Ornaghi, V. (2020). Mental health promotion in schools: A comprehensive theoretical framework. *International Journal of Emotional Education, 12*(1), 65–82.

Cavioni, V., Grazzani, V., Ornaghi, V., Agliati, A., Gandellini, S., Cefai, C., et al. (2023a). A multi-component curriculum to promote teachers' mental health: Findings from the PROMEHS program. *International Journal of Emotional Education, 15*(1), 34–52. https://doi.org/10.56300/KFNZ2526

Cavioni, V., Toto, G., & Ornaghi, V. (2023b). Portraits of pre-service special education teachers: Clustered perspectives on their well-being and its association with self-efficacy and commitment to work. *International Journal of Emotional Education, 15*(2), 21–36. https://doi.org/10.56300/VHRV8364

Cavioni, V., Ornaghi, V., & Conte, E. (2024). Promoting teachers' well-being through a serious game intervention: A qualitative exploration of teachers' experiences. *Frontiers in Psychology, 15*, 1339242. https://doi.org/10.3389/fpsyg.2024.1339242

Cefai, C., & Cavioni, V. (2014). *Social and emotional education in primary school: Integrating theory and research into practice*. Springer.

Cefai, C., Simões, C., & Caravita, S. (2021). *A systemic, whole-school approach to mental health and well-being in schools in the EU. NESET report*. Publications Office of the European Union.

Cefai, C., Camilleri, L., Bartolo, P., Grazzani, I., Cavioni, V., Conte, E., et al. (2022). The effectiveness of a school-based, universal mental health programme in six European countries. *Frontiers in Psychology, 13*, 925614. https://doi.org/10.3389/fpsyg.2022.925614

Chen, M.-F., Chen, Y.-C., Zuo, P.-Y., & Hou, H.-T. (2023). Design and evaluation of a remote synchronous gamified mathematics teaching activity that integrates multi-representational scaffolding and a mind tool for gamified learning. *Education and Information Technologies, 28*, 11708–11706. https://doi.org/10.1007/s10639-023-11708-6

Cichy, I., Kaczmarczyk, M., Wawrzyniak, S., Kruszwicka, A., Przybyla, T., Klichowski, M., & Rokita, A. (2020). Participating in physical classes using Eduball stimulates acquisition of mathematical knowledge and skills by primary school students. *Frontiers in Psychology, 11*, 2194. https://doi.org/10.3389/fpsyg.2020.02194

Cipriano, C., Strambler, M. J., Naples, L. H., Ha, C., Kirk, M., Wood, M., et al. (2023). The state of evidence for social and emotional learning: A contemporary meta-analysis of universal school-based SEL interventions. *Child Development, 94*(5), 1181–1204. https://doi.org/10.1111/cdev.13968

Connor, K. M., & Davidson, J. R. T. (2003). Development of a new resilience scale: The Connor-Davidson Resilience Scale (CD-RISC). *Depression and Anxiety, 18*(2), 76–82. https://doi.org/10.1002/da.10113

Conte, E., Cavioni, V., Ornaghi, V., Agliati, A., Gandellini, S., Frade Santos, M., et al. (2023). Supporting preschoolers' mental health and academic learning through the PROMEHS program: A training study. *Children, 10*(6), 1070. https://doi.org/10.3390/children10061070

Denham, S. A., Bassett, H. H., & Zinsser, K. (2012). Early childhood teachers as socializers of young children's emotional competence. *Early Childhood Education Journal, 40*(3), 137–143. https://doi.org/10.1007/s10643-012-0504-2

Deterding, S. (2012). Gamification: Designing for motivation. *Interactions, 19*(4), 14–17. https://doi.org/10.1145/2212877.2212883

Durlak, J. A., Dymnicki, A. B., Taylor, R. D., & Schellinger, K. B. (2011). The impact of enhancing students' social and emotional learning: A meta-analysis of school-based universal interventions. *Child Development, 82*(1), 405–432. https://doi.org/10.1111/j.1467-8624.2010.01564.x

Faiella, F., & Ricciardi, M. (2015). Gamification and learning: A review of issues and research. *Journal of E-Learning and Knowledge Society, 11*(3). https://doi.org/10.20368/1971-8829/107

Grazzani, I., Agliati, A., Conte, E., Cavioni, V., Gandellini, S., Ornaghi, V., et al. (2022). *PROMEHS. The curriculum to promote mental health at school. Activities handbook for teacher, Kindergarten and Primary school (Ages 3–10).* Mimesis Edizioni. ISBN: 978-88-5758-958-9.

Grazzani, I., Martinsone, B., Simoes, C., Cavioni, V., Conte, E., Ornaghi, V., & Pepe, A. (2024). Assessing teachers' social and emotional competence: The validation of SECTRS in Italy, Latvia, and Portugal. *International Journal of Emotional Education, 16*(1), 70–87. https://doi.org/10.56300/QIAN8168

Jennings, P. A., Brown, J. L., Frank, J. L., Doyle, S., Oh, Y., Davis, R., & Greenberg, M. T. (2017). Impacts of the CARE for teachers program on teachers' social and emotional competence and classroom interactions. *Journal of Educational Psychology, 109*(7), 1010–1028. https://doi.org/10.1037/edu0000187

Jorm, A. F., Korten, A. E., Jacomb, P. A., Christensen, H., Rodgers, B., & Pollitt, P. (1997). Mental health literacy: A survey of the public's ability to recognise mental disorders and their beliefs about the effectiveness of treatment. *The Medical Journal of Australia, 166*(4), 182–186. https://doi.org/10.5694/j.1326-5377.1997.tb140071.x

Nalipay, M. J. N., King, R. B., Haw, J. Y., Mordeno, I. G., & Dela Rosa, E. D. (2021). Teachers who believe that emotions are changeable are more positive and engaged: The role of emotion mindset among in- and preservice teachers. *Learning and Individual Differences, 92*, 102050. https://doi.org/10.1016/j.lindif.2021.102050

OECD—Organization for Economic Co-operation and Development. (2024). Engaging learners: Fostering inclusion through well-being and mental health supports. In *Proceedings of the 11th Policy Forum*. OECD. Retrieved January 14, 2025, https://www.oecd.org/content/dam/oecd/en/about/projects/edu/education-for-inclusive-societies/Forum_Proceedings_11th_Policy_Forum_2024.pdf

Parker, B. L., Anderson, M., Batterham, P. J., Gayed, A., Subotic-Kerry, M., Achilles, et al. (2021). Examining the preliminary effectiveness and acceptability of a web-based training program for Australian secondary school teachers: Pilot study of the BEAM (Building Educators' Skills in Adolescent Mental Health) program. *JMIR Mental Health, 8*(10), e29989. https://doi.org/10.2196/2998

Patalay, P., & Fitzsimons, E. (2018). Development and predictors of mental ill-health and wellbeing from childhood to adolescence. *Social Psychiatry and Psychiatric Epidemiology, 53*(12), 1311–1323. https://doi.org/10.1007/s00127-018-1604-0

Persico, D., Manganello, F., Passarelli, M., & Pozzi, F. (2023). Is GBL good for teachers? A game for teachers on how to foster students' self-regulated learning. *Education Sciences, 13*, 1180. https://doi.org/10.3390/educsci13121180

Sailer, M., Hense, J. U., Mayr, S. K., & Mandl, H. (2017). How gamification motivates: An experimental study of the effects of specific game design elements on psychological need satisfaction. *Computers in Human Behavior, 69*, 371–380. https://doi.org/10.1016/j.chb.2016.12.033

Talič, A., Bogdan Zupančič, A., Avguštin, L., Beržanskytė, J., Šukytė, D., Širokova, M., et al. (2023). *Teaching To Be: A Path to Wellbeing. Teacher workbook*. Self-published.
Tom, K. M. (2012). *Measurement of teachers' social-emotional competence: Development of the social-emotional competence teacher rating scale* [Doctoral dissertation]. Retrieved January 11, 2025, from https://scholarsbank.uoregon.edu/xmlui/bitstream/handle/1794/12351/Tom_oregon_0171A_10250.pdf?sequence=1&isAllowed=y
Tschannen-Moran, M., & Woolfolk Hoy, A. (2001). Teacher efficacy: Capturing an elusive construct. *Teaching and Teacher Education, 17*(7), 783–805. https://doi.org/10.1016/S0742-051X(01)00036-1
Weare, K., & Nind, M. (2011). Mental health promotion and problem prevention in schools: What does the evidence say? *Health Promotion International, 26*(1), i29–i69. https://doi.org/10.1093/heapro/dar075
Weston, K., Ott, M., & Rodger, S. (2018). Yet one more expectation for teachers. In A. W. Leschied, D. H. Saklofske, & G. L. Flett (Eds.), *Handbook of school-based mental health promotion. An evidence-informed framework for implementation* (pp. 105–126). Springer.
Yamaguchi, S., Foo, J. C., Kitagawa, Y., Togo, F., & Sasaki, T. (2021). A survey of mental health literacy in Japanese high school teachers. *BMC Psychiatry, 21*(1), 478. https://doi.org/10.1186/s12888-021-03481-y
Yañez, A. G. B., Alonso-Fernández, C., Pérez-Colado, V. M., & Fernández-Manjón, B. (2023). Blue is for boys and pink is for girls: How to break gender stereotypes with a videogame. *Education Sciences, 13*, 1004. https://doi.org/10.3390/educsci13101004

Index[1]

[1] Note: Page numbers followed by 'n' refer to notes.

V. Cavioni, *Fostering Teachers' Mental Health*,
https://doi.org/10.1007/978-3-031-92571-9